Festina Lente

Thriving in the Shadow of Giants

Thriving in the Shadow of Giants

*How to Find Success
as an Independent Retailer*

Eddy Kay

The Armarium Press Inc.
West Hollywood, California

Festina lente, the crab and butterfly woodcut, Good News About, and Mr. Goodnews are registered trademarks of The Armarium Press Inc. on file with the U.S. Patent and Trademark Office. All other brand and product names used in this book are trade names, service marks, trademarks, or registered trademarks of their respective owners.

Printing History
2 4 6 8 10 9 7 5 3
First Edition February 2002
Copyright© 2002 by Eddy Kay

All rights reserved.

No part of this book may be reproduced or transmitted in any form or by any means, electronic or mechanical, including photocopying, recording, or by any information storage or retrieval system, without prior permission in writing from The Armarium Press, except for brief quotations used in a review.

ISBN: 0-9707825-0-0

Cover design by Jean-Paul Duberg.
Illustrations by Emma Stephens Larson.
Logo woodcut by Matthew Grogan.
Research assistance by Erin Mulholland.

Printed in the United States of America.

THE ARMARIUM PRESS.
8391 BEVERLY BOULEVARD, NO. 451
WEST HOLLYWOOD, CALIFORNIA 90048
www.TheArmariumPress.com

Acknowledgements

I'd like to thank my wife, Michielle, for proofreading every page I have written for the last 30 years. Thanks to my editor, Robyn McCarthy, for proofreading every page thereafter. Thanks to my publisher, Carmen Madrid, for camping out in my kitchen until this book was finished. And a final thanks to Brian McCarthy, who is responsible for you holding this book in your hands.

"All things being equal, I'll buy at the cheapest place."

*This book is dedicated to Al Brotsky,
the greatest retailer I've ever known*

Table of Contents

	Foreword	xi
Chapter 1	Time for a Retail Reality Check	15
Chapter 2	Evolution – It's Not Just a Theory *Specialist Spotlight on The Fret House*	19
Chapter 3	Just Who Are Mom and Pop? *Specialist Spotlight on Di-No Computers*	29
Chapter 4	Where Has All the Service Gone? *Specialist Spotlight on Covina Valley Schwinn*	39
Chapter 5	All Things Being Equal, I'll Buy at the Cheapest Place *Specialist Spotlight on L&W Appliance*	59
Chapter 6	Reviving Your Personal Trade *Specialist Spotlight on Borgman's Jewelers*	71
Chapter 7	Selling the Good Stuff *Specialist Spotlight on Logan's Hardware*	79
Chapter 8	Learning to Lead! *Specialist Spotlight on Allied Model Trains*	89
Chapter 9	There's Nothing Casual About Business *Specialist Spotlight on Insane Stereo*	101
Chapter 10	Getting the Word Out *Specialist Spotlight on Clues Unlimited*	111
Chapter 11	Good News About Retailing	125
	Index	130

Foreword

Nothing happens until somebody sells something. This is an oft-repeated truism in business. Yet it also reflects why independent retailers are so important. As Eddy Kay knows so well, independent retailers are the lifeblood of new products coming to market. A potential customer must feel comfortable with a retailer before he buys any product – especially those items and technologies that are new to market.

Such products require an explanation. They require a relationship. They require trust. Whether they're shopping for HDTV or a computer, a riding mower or a boat, jewelry or furniture, people want to buy smart – and they need to trust the retailer that they are buying the right product for their needs.

The last century's history of retailing is a tale of the new threatening the old. At the turn of the 20th century we had the Montgomery Ward catalog… In the 1950s we saw the growth of Sears… Federated and Kmart took the lead in the 1970s… Wal-Mart and the "power retailers" made their presence felt in the 1990s. Most recently, Amazon.com and other "pure Internet" retailers have guided retailing in a new direction.

Ultimately, though, what makes a difference is not a retailer's size, its methods of distribution, or even its products. What makes a difference is a staff's training, its relationship with customers, and the trust built between them.

Eddy Kay knows this. He has a phenomenal reputation for giving retailers the training they need to earn customers' trust and, thereby, succeed in a competitive marketplace. His unique experience, wit, insights, and proven training program have made a difference for hundreds of store owners.

Thriving in the Shadow of Giants takes Eddy's famous training program one step farther – by serving as a "wake-up" call for business owners who've become complacent about moderate success. This book also offers a survival-school course for those prone to complaining they're being driven out of business by the big guys.

It is a scary environment for independent specialists. A tough economy and competition from Internet retailers, discounters, and superstores make it seem the independent retailer faces impossible odds. Yet this intense competition not only benefits consumers with price, quality, and service choice, it makes all the competitors better by forcing each of them to focus on what they do best.

For independent retailers, local knowledge and the trust of their increasingly time-pressured customers can help give them the edge over other retailers. Eddy's message is that small business owners must recognize and use their natural advantages.

One of Eddy's broadest audiences each year is at the International Consumer Electronics Show. This event, the world's largest consumer technology gathering, attracts more than 120,000 retailers, journalists, and government officials to Las Vegas each January. Exhibitors launch new products and gauge retailers' reaction to them against a backdrop of dynamic merchandising displays. An exhibiting company's success for the entire year may depend on whether they are able to pique the interest of visiting retailers in selling their new product.

As both a speaker and motivator, Eddy's role at this exciting annual event is significant. If small business owners leave CES re-energized, with new ideas and a healthy attitude, then consumers will buy and the industry succeeds.

So the industry is happy when Eddy and his converts take to the road. Teaching, training, and helping retailers succeed is the protein in his diet.

And now that there is a book, we're all excited. Eddy's insights memorialized in print not only provide a great read, they will make any reader in retail a better competitor.

Gary Shapiro, President & CEO
Consumer Electronics Association

Chapter 1
Time for a Retail Reality Check

I've been in retail for more than 20 years. I was one of those people who didn't know how to do anything. So, I got a job in sales. I figured, how hard could it be? The people who wait on me now don't know anything. I don't know anything. Therefore, I'm qualified. This absurd presumption was verified by the fact someone hired me. My training was similar to most retail training: They told me what time to show up, pointed to the sales floor, and told me to go for it.

Being a man of intense energy, combined with the fact my family needed steady meals, I did okay. In this case, "okay" means I made a living. I had no choice – the rent was due. In retrospect, I realize I wasn't doing as well as I thought. Because I was making a living, I assumed I knew what I was doing. In fact, I was leaving a third of what was available behind. Because I had the highest numbers in the store, I thought I was the best. In reality, I was just failing the least.

That realization hit me like a glass of cold water in my face. I was shocked by how much I obviously did not know about what I did for a living. I realized retail is not simply a roll of the dice – that it can indeed be done with purpose. But what scared me the most was the thought that everyone around me understood retail but me.

I panicked. I decided that if I were to stay in retail, I'd better know more about this business. I studied, I learned… and among my newfound nuggets of knowledge was the fact that retail is actually *not* about price. What a surprise! Price was all I'd ever heard retailers talk about. And apparently customer service doesn't simply mean waiting on a shopper as soon as possible. It turned out there were scores of customer service issues I'd never even considered. Through innocence and ignorance, I was impeding my own growth while looking for a bad guy to blame my problems on.

Most specialist retailers today are in the same boat I was in those many years ago. Only today it's much easier to find someone to blame for your problems. The bad guys are so huge you can't help but see them in your scopes.

So just who *is* killing the little guy's profits, stealing his customers, and preventing peace in the Middle East? The retail superstores, of course!

The superstore and its online counterparts have become the perfect excuse for failure. What so many specialist retailers don't realize is that the superstore is the best thing to happen to them since they opened their doors. It's just a matter of knowing how to compete in the areas the superstore cannot.

The superstores offer little service or product knowledge. They have enormous staffs with continuous turnover. There are exceptions, but for the most part what I'm saying is true. Anyone who works at a superstore long enough to obtain any expertise gets promoted to manager. When that happens, the store has lost its best salesperson and has acquired another rookie manager.

This is where you, the independent retailer, have your greatest opportunity. While the superstore is trying to lick a wound it can't reach, you're able to act. And that's what this book is all about: how to act – and act now... how to recognize opportunities and take them... how to thrive and not simply survive.

Don't think for a second that superstore executives don't want to accomplish the same thing. They do. But because their crews are selling squat and having no fun to boot, their turnover is tremendous. They never have the chance to create a genuine sales team.

Now Circuit City, Sears, Wal-Mart, Best Buy, and The Home Depot did not get hundreds of stores apiece because their top brass are poor businesspeople. These guys are terrific! Yet because they can't count on their salespeople for growth, they have to do retail differently. And they're great at it. But try to do it the way the giants do – by competing on price and selection – and you'll get killed.

You'll find no excuses for failure in these pages – just the tools you need to succeed. Keep in mind that just because the superstores are not your biggest problem today, doesn't mean you *don't* have to change the way you've been doing business. Retail evolves – and if you're satisfied to run your business today the way you did 10 or 20 years ago, sure, you're going to be in for some tough times. 1985 is never coming back.

Blaming your woes on someone else isn't going to change anything. Learning how to capitalize on your differences from the big guys is. Besides, looking for excuses isn't really the mark of a leader.

This book will help you create those things that make your store a desirable place to shop. The Specialist Spotlight at the end of each chapter profiles independent retailers already thriving, not just surviving. Learn from their examples. (I also illustrate what *not* to do with tales of my personal shopping nightmares – many of which I'm sure you've experienced as a consumer yourself. Even as you laugh, ask yourself whether customers could *ever* have such an experience in your store.)

Envision your store as a place where customer service is the attitude, not a job. A place with an ongoing and self-perpetuating corporate culture. A place where everyone learns from everybody else – and what they're learning is exactly what you, the owner or manager, wants them to learn. A place like The Ritz-Carlton Hotels.

At $325 a night, I can't afford to stay at the Ritz-Carlton, but a client put me up there once. On my way to the lobby, I saw housekeeping servicing a room. I paused in the open door and asked the maid where Ballroom C was. Without hesitation, she stopped what she was doing, closed the room, and escorted me there. I told her it wasn't necessary. She said she was happy to do so. In my mind, I was keeping her from doing her job. In her mind, that's exactly what she was doing. The room could wait. Her customer could not. That attitude is the thread and fabric of that organization. It's what makes the hotel a value to those who can afford to stay there.

Contrast this experience with a $60 a night hotel. There, the maid knocks on the door and asks if she can come in and clean up. She comes in, takes a shower, and leaves. That's the $265 difference.

I'm going to show you how to instill a Ritz-Carlton kind of attitude in your store. I will teach you how to create it and maintain it. I do this in self-defense. I want to shop at your store. I want to give you all my money. And I'm not alone. There are hundreds of thousands of folks just like me. And they're all looking for a place like… yours?

Chapter 2
Evolution — It's Not Just a Theory

The evolution of retailing mirrors the evolution of society itself. The human condition seems to compel us to possess stuff – lots of it. And wouldn't it be cool if we could get all this stuff we want in a single location? The answer is yes. And for the last 5,000 years we've been trying to accomplish just that.

Wait, I know what you're thinking… Moldy old history has nothing to teach me about running my business at the start of the 21st century. Let me say two things. First, evolution is ongoing… in retailing as much as in nature. Second, complacency has destroyed many a good business concept. As I mentioned in the previous chapter, it's time to stop worrying about the retail giants as your direct competition. Yet that bit of good news doesn't mean you should continue doing business the same way you always have. There's no crying in baseball, and no resting on your laurels in retail.

Understanding how the business has evolved throughout the centuries will help you recognize how it continues to change. Understanding the roots of specialist retailing will help you get back to them. On with our history lesson.…

The concept of retail was pretty much established by 3,000 B.C. In those primitive days, retail stores took the form of open-air bazaars. Today we call them outdoor flea markets. People would gather in a central location, park their camels, and barter for goods. Unlike today's retailers, however, those "store owners" actually manufactured the goods they sold. They had no salespeople. I recall from my college history classes that several hundred years later in China, salespeople were looked down upon as the scum of society. They offered nothing and lived off the work of others. (It hurts me to say this, but things haven't changed much over the past five millennia.)

In the classical Greek and Roman periods, the salesperson's social stature grew. Others dirtied their hands while the merchant took care of business. But these men dealt in such commodities as slaves, grain, and building materials. Artisan goods – shoes, weapons, togas – were still manufactured by the same people who sold them. Those open-air markets were very well organized, however. Although the stores were actually tents, one could count on finding the tent in the same place every time you went shopping. Of course, the shopping district moved from place to place....

By the 14th century, we see retail taking on a more recognizable form. As neighborhoods became more "in vogue," permanent shops became a common occurrence. You could find yourself a butcher, a baker, and a candlestick maker in the same location year after year.

Come the end of the 18th century, the concept of wholesale was in force. A shoemaker no longer had to deal with his local slaughterhouse for hide. He could buy it from a distributor who, for a price, would deliver it tanned and ready to go. This saved an enormous amount of time, enabling the merchant to produce more goods. Increased production led to more sales and a better life for the shoemaker.

The 19th century Industrial Revolution made goods so cheap that the common man could finally buy items once affordable only to the elite. Production could not keep up with demand. Retailers thrived. Not only was business great, but every day some new invention appeared – the sewing machine, the cotton gin, Sears' Bust Enlargement Cream.... This led to new demand and new specialists to fill the pipeline.

The market eventually grew beyond the retail store. Rural America had a hard time making it to town, since "town" was often 100 miles away in an age when 30 miles was a long day's journey. The farmer didn't mind, but it was murder on the horse. Besides, it took too much time. What farmer can leave his farm for a week at a time just to do a little shopping? These rural customers could always wait for the "traveling salesman" to come a-knockin' on their doors, but not every salesman sold what you needed on that particular day. And once a farmer ran out of daughters, the salesmen seldom came back anyway.

In 1872, Aaron Montgomery Ward changed the face of shopping forever with the invention of "mail order retailing." He decided if the customer could not get to town, the town would go to the customer.

That first Montgomery Ward catalog was a virtual superstore by today's standards. It carried almost everything imaginable. In 1886, Sears Roebuck & Co. became the world's second superstore, emulating Montgomery Ward with equal success.

Yet these retailing pioneers realized after a while that not all customers wanted to do their shopping by mail. They liked the ease of finding everything they needed in one place, but frowned on the inconvenience. Clothes didn't fit right. Appliances didn't look like their catalog pictures. If the tires didn't fit your model T, it took too long for an exchange. And what about the cost of shipping?!

If you got knocked out wearing your new boxing gloves, would the company give you a new pair? Worse yet, what if your new hay tedder arrived when the sun wasn't shining? For $29 though, Sears offered a "Boys All-Steel Velocipede" that couldn't be beat.

What these companies needed was a real store. In order to have a brick and mortar store that sold the kind of variety available in the catalogs,

> If the customer couldn't get to town, the town would go to the customer.

however, it would have to be the size of Toledo. So in 1920, Sears Roebuck & Co. opened their main retail outlet and company headquarters in downtown Chicago. The place was enormous: 12 stories high and occupying a square city block, it was the largest retail store in the world. It sold everything from groceries to automobiles, even homes for which it held the mortgages. For many, many years, Sears was "Where America Shops."

The superstore has taken on many different names and descriptions since then. The modern version is a single-site operation that carries a multitude of items in a single category: an appliance superstore or an electronics superstore. They feature state-of-the-art equipment, merchandising techniques, and superior service. Staff members are knowledgeable and professional. It's a Mom and Pop Shop on steroids – the ultimate specialty store.

Unfortunately, few such stores remain anywhere. Most have been replaced by the "Big Box Retailers" – you know, the giant chains that sell an enormous amount of volume at discount prices. Office Depot. Circuit City. IKEA. PetSmart. These are the Goliaths of today. When I say superstore, these are the guys I'm talking about. These industry giants have redefined retail. Although they have lost the ability to provide many of the services provided by the Mom and Pops, they have earned a chunk of the market that belongs to them alone.

These Goliaths offer consumers multi-tiered product selection. If you want a new stove, you can choose from three different lines: a good line, a better line, and a top-of-the-line line. Moreover, you'll find a "good, better, best" choice within each of those lines. So you've got nine different models to choose from. Multiply that figure by the number of home appliances available, and you'll have a superstore indeed. It takes a warehouse the size of New Jersey just to house the inventory. The independent retailer simply can't afford such an investment. The superstores can, because they have Goliath-size advertising budgets to bring a tremendous number of shoppers through their doors. The independent specialist gets the leftovers.

Yet the leftovers in this case could feed a couple of armies. The superstores do not just advertise for themselves. They advertise for the little guy as well. When the superstores draw these customers into the market, where do you think they go when they don't make a purchase at the first place they stop? Maybe to another superstore… maybe to you.

Yes, independent retailers have a terrific opportunity today – if they can learn how to exploit it. You can take advantage of this reality, or you can stand in the path of retail evolution, yelling "Stop!" about as effectively as someone trying to halt a hurricane. It's a new century – it's time for a new attitude about change.

Specialist Spotlight on... The Fret House

Tom Seymour is a man of change who doesn't appear to change at all. Tall and thin, he wears a grey-white beard and ponytail. If 1965 ever comes back, Tom's ready to go. He looks like he should be selling folk music to hippies. For years he did. And although most of those hippies are gone, Tom still sells guitars to the neighborhood. He's been around for 31 years.

The Fret House is a single-store operation. People know Tom, and they like him. His gentle manner comes as no surprise: He's been a second-grade teacher for longer than he's owned the store. "Seven-year-olds are a delightful way to spend your days," he says with a twinkle in his eye. When the school day is over, Tom heads for his shop.

Although Tom isn't there to open in the morning, the place is in good hands. His manager has been with him for 23 years. The two other full-time employees have been there 10 and 12 years. Even the part-time staff members are old-timers by retail standards. He's got two right now who've worked at The Fret House for three years. (About 18 months is the retail industry standard.) "It's a nice job to have while you're in college," Tom says.

How does he maintain this incredibly low turnover rate? "Fun is the number one factor in any company's success," he says. All of his employees play the guitar. They love to show 'em, hold 'em, play 'em, and sell 'em. And they really know their stuff. It takes about two years of training before the team will actually consider a newcomer one of the family.

During that period, the novitiate learns construction, finish, function, repair, and history of the instrument. Any one of Tom's guys can tell you the year a guitar was made by its serial number. We're talking genuine "product knowledge" here. In Tom's store you don't speak as an expert unless you are one. These guys know banjos, dulcimers, mandolins, violins, horns, and reeds.

The Fret House is one cool shop. It's also a mile away from Guitar Center, the largest musical instrument superstore chain in the world.

Guitar Center is one of the music industry's big three, with Mars and Sam Ash. At least one of these companies dominates every market they're in. Their stores are clean, wonderfully merchandised, filled with light, and a blast to be in. With 30,000 square feet filled to the brim with merchandise, they're hard to beat for selection and price. They carry everything Tom carries and sell it for less.

When Guitar Center moved into the area 15 years ago, Tom felt the effect immediately. He could match the company's prices but, like any independent, he couldn't buy as sharp. This resulted in lower margins. Tom still sold the same amount as before, but he wasn't making as much money. That's a bad thing.

But Tom has an attitude – a good one. He says he walks into the store every day as if it's his first day in business. He realizes today is already gone, and tomorrow the world will be a different place. You have to change to accommodate it.

It's not just a way of business with Tom. It's a way of life. As he sees it, continuous change keeps you fresh, creative, and bright.

It also put his little guitar shop in a perfect position to stand up to the giant down the street. Tom and his team knew they couldn't make their living just selling musical instruments any more. They had to look for the market holes a superstore couldn't fill. They found a number of them.

First, the Guitar Center near him doesn't give music lessons. If you want to learn how to play the instrument you just bought, you'll have to go someplace else. Tom doesn't mind: He's always had teachers on staff. With the increased number of players thanks to all the sales the superstore was making, he had to beef up his teaching staff. Teaching may not be a great profit center, but students spend a ton of money on the peripherals. That's a good thing.

Tom also employs a full-time luthier, who not only repairs but actually sets up new guitars. Guitars arrive from the manufacturer requiring minor adjustments to make them play just right for each new owner's taste and musical style.

Superstores generally send customers out to have this fine-tuning done. Many of them find their way to The Fret House. Tom doesn't make a killing from fine-tuning and repairing instruments. Yet he does bring in a steady stream of customers by offering highly personalized service in an area where the big guys simply cannot compete.

Tom also understands the guitar players' psyche – how they just love fancy instruments. With hand-selected exotic woods and magnificent abalone inlay, some of these beauties will sell for as much as $16,000. In many cases, they're one of a kind.

He keeps a few such instruments on display at any given time, in a glass case to keep off the drool as customers dream of owning such a work of art. A new model will create a buzz among local musicians, drawing them into the store.

Sometimes these guitars sell the first week. Others stay for years. Either way, they make a positive statement, defining for long-time customers and newcomers alike exactly what The Fret House is all about. The superstores cannot carry such instruments because they don't turn fast enough. Besides, you can't really have an identical "one of a kind" guitar in each of your stores.

But wait! There's more… The superstores don't always do business with local schools. So, where do the kids get all those shiny instruments? At Tom's, of course. The same parents rent the clarinet and four years later buy the guitar.

Yes, Tom thrives just fine in the shadow of his industry's giant retailers. In fact, he plans to retire from teaching next year and work in the store full time. The first item on his to-do list is to move the business into a larger building. He envisions the repair shop in his front window, so passers-by can watch his craftsmen at work.

After the change to the larger building will come new ideas about reaching out to and servicing his customers. Yet while the location change will allow him to discover new ways to compete, some things are sure to remain the same: Tom will still come to work, full beard and ponytail, put the key in the door, and congratulate himself on his first day in business.

Chapter 3
Just Who Are Mom and Pop?

As the folks at The Fret House showed us, adapting to an evolving marketplace requires you to anticipate and embrace change. You must seek out those little niches of customer service where the big guys cannot evolve because they're just too big. Yet thriving in the shadow of giants means looking backwards for inspiration, as well as ahead. As an independent specialist, you must never forget who you are and how you got there.

When you started the business (or when your parents started the business), life was easy. If you owned a butcher shop, no supermarket chains threatened you. If you sold clothing, you didn't fear a Men's Wearhouse moving into the neighborhood. If televisions were your business, you probably sold washing machines too. Wal-Mart wasn't a concern. As a specialist, you offered merchandise and knowledge customers could count on. When customers came in, you probably knew their names. You saw them all the time. You remembered what they bought on their previous visits and could recommend new items to go with the old. The "salesperson" was usually the owner or someone in the family. Hence the name "Mom and Pop."

Today we call these folks "the independents." These are the husbands and wives who quit their jobs and put their houses on the line for a better future. They borrowed from their parents, the bank, and their friends. They went out on a limb so fragile the slightest breeze could send them for a tumble.

I know a man who made good on every one of those "pre-approved" credit card applications. He and his wife actually accumulated $50,000 worth of credit, at usury rates, to begin their business. They are good, honest people. But all they need is 90 bad business days in a row and they're history. They will lose everything they have, face paying off that debt for years to come, and never get over the embarrassment of failure. And for the most part, the only business plan they put together was based on a dream.

Most new store owners have no retail experience. They think they're the Little Rascals: "Hey, let's put on a show!" "Yeah, I've got a guitar." "And I've got a barn." "Let's go!"

In the next scene, all the sets are built. The barn animals are the motors for all the mechanical devices, raising the curtain and propelling the vehicles. The contraptions that run the event have been engineered by seven-year-olds with degrees from MIT. A hand-drawn sign on the front of the barn announces that the show starts at three o'clock that afternoon. Come three o'clock the place is filled with youngsters carrying an endless supply of rotten fruits and vegetables to throw at the stage. The show is a hit, and the audience offers a standing ovation. The kids did it themselves. And they did it in just four hours.

Think I'm exaggerating? Let's consider a real-world example of Little Rascal thinking. A neighbor of ours some years ago opened a sporting goods place about six blocks from the house. His plan? To undersell the superstores: "We'll be so cheap no one will ever shop at those guys again." I asked how he would survive with no detectable profit margin. He showed me a catalog from a sporting goods manufacturer located in Mainland China. "I can get everything I need from these guys," he said. "Look, a $35 backpack for $3. I'll sell it for 15 bucks. The superstores have nothing like it."

Since he had already signed a lease, I didn't have the heart to tell him something was wrong with his picture. He had no other plan than "sell it cheap and people will find you." So, as long as he was "in the business," I figured I could get a backpack for my son. He sold me one at cost – $3. When my son put his books in it, the seam in the bottom of the bag opened like the Red Sea. I took it back, and he gave me another. Then another. I would have gotten a fourth had a windstorm not blown the store's new $2,000 sign to smithereens.

Within two weeks he closed the shop, claiming that retail is too much trouble. Part of the problem was that he was an absentee owner. He had another job and was never in the store. He let his son run it. Believe me when I tell you that no one will protect your investment like you will. What he should have done was rent a barn. At three o'clock he would have had a store filled with customers holding fruits and vegetables of the same quality as the goods he sold.

So, I guess being the cheapest isn't the answer. If you're going to be the most expensive, though, you must give the customer more than just good merchandise. You must give them *added value*. And only two people in the world can give the kind of added value you need to thrive alongside the superstore: Mom and Pop.

Watch some old TV shows and you'll get the idea. If you remember the Dobie Gillis show from the 1950s and early '60s (or watch Nick at Nite), you'll know that Dobie's parents owned a neighborhood grocery and lived in an apartment upstairs. They knew their customers' names and suggested foods to fit their tastes and lifestyles. It was a business built on personal relationships.

I know. My grandparents owned a grocery store during the Depression. In fact, they supported the neighborhood with credit before the concept of credit cards or personal collateral was a household word. No one was going to skip on his bill. There was no place to skip to. What would he do… run to another house and hide his 10 kids?

> You must give customers more than just good merchandise. You must give them *added value*.

My grandparents were still running that store when I came along in the 1950s. A small shop with floors of wooden slats, dark and dank, it smelled like a meat market. The front door, with a screen door just like at home, was always open to let in more light. Towering about twice as high as my little boy self, a display of cans dominated the middle of the room. "Don't go near those cans!" they always yelled at me. "You'll shoot your eye out!" I remember gawking at the dead chickens hanging behind the counter. Even at seven years old, I realized they weren't going back to their Bugs Bunny cartoon. And besides, that couldn't be where fried chicken came from.

I can picture the time a lady walked in with a grocery list in her hand as clearly as if it were yesterday: "Mrs. Solomon!" my grandfather greets her. "How are you, my dear? And how are the twins, Jackie and Alan? Wonderful, wonderful. How's Mr. Solomon's feet? Getting better I hope. Can I get you more of the Epsom salt? It seemed to give him some relief the last time."

The elderly woman (she was probably 40) sighs and offers the latest news about the neighbors. Gossip, a basic ingredient in the shopping ritual, involved everyone. My mother nods her head in disbelief and agrees at every turn. My grandfather slaps his forehead at the appropriate moments. My grandmother is in the back unloading a semi by herself and thanking God for the opportunity. These were a different kind of people.

After they all agree that life is hard and that God had blessed them, Mrs. Solomon hands my grandfather her list. He turns to get a giant empty box with Oxydol printed on the side and starts to fill it up. Every so often he gets this huge clamp contraption with a broom handle on it. He reaches way up to the top shelf, pulls the string, and brings down a box of corn flakes trapped in its jaws. He clamps another box, and then another. It takes him 15 minutes to fill the order. Then he carries the groceries out to Mrs. Solomon's car.

When my grandparents retired in 1960, they closed the store. No one wanted to buy it. The supermarket had arrived, and no one had the insight to see that all a supermarket could provide was food. The intangibles that breed loyalty, community, and a sense of well-being were cast aside in favor of convenience.

Specialist Spotlight on...

Di-No Computers

Believe it or not, Sal Cordaro grew up living over his parents' grocery store. He was the Dobie Gillis of his day, with one major exception – Dobie never played the organ; Sal does. At 15, Sal began playing the organ professionally. He played his way to college. He played his way to becoming a chemical engineer. Since playing music was more fun than playing with chemicals, he played his way to becoming the house musician in the same nightclub for more than 20 years. As they say in the business, "he owned the room." Sal also sat in with some of the greatest names of the Big Band era. He's definitely the real thing.

On top of his gig at the club, Sal sold organs and taught music at a local music store. Since his parents actually were Mom and Pop, it was natural for him to bring along those values when he had customers of his own.

Like all musicians, Sal loved to hear himself on tape. And, like most players, he owned as much recording equipment as his marriage would allow. In fact, he had so much equipment, he eventually gave birth to Di-No Records. The company was named after his two most fervent supporters: his daughters Diane and Noreen. Sal was the label's number one star and produced the records he sold at the club.

Sal was indeed a 20th century man. If it plugged into the wall and did magic, he wanted it. In the early days of microcomputers, the space-age technology fascinated him. A computer in your home – that actually fits on a single desk? Remarkable! Remember the scene in *Apollo 13* when Jim Lovell talks about believing in the impossible, such as a computer that fits in a single room? Sal is no less awed by new technology and how it works. He was passionate about getting one of the new desktop gizmos. You don't find a lot of passion in a superstore.

One eventful day, an employee from the Jet Propulsion Laboratory happened into the store and spotted Sal playing with his new toy. "Hey, where can I get one of those?" the man asked. Sal thought for a moment and realized he could buy one and resell it to this man. "Why, right here!" Sal replied and sold the man a computer on the spot. In fact, Sal sold computers to most of the man's rocket scientist friends. Within six months he'd opened a computer department inside the music store. Soon after, he split the department off as its own company.

Twenty-three years later, Di-No Computers is doing great. It's bright, full of activity, and you can almost hear a buzz of excitement when you walk through the doors. Sal's passion for electronic gadgets permeates the place. Employees stay with Di-No for a minimum of six years, and their intense interest in the products they sell shines through to customers.

Their clients come from a rainbow of vocations, keeping the sales experience fresh and the challenges new. The fact that Di-No only sells Macintosh equipment makes the personal touch even more important. With most people out there using PCs, Mac customers can't get help from their "expert" computer friends.

You see, the people who work at Di-No Computers realize that computers aren't like most commodities. When you buy a vest at The Gap, you don't have to call for instructions on buttoning it up. Computers don't run themselves. They often don't work even when you know how to use them, and sometimes they don't work when they're not even broken. We've all heard the line: "There's nothing wrong with your computer. It's a software problem." How comforting is that to someone who's just spent $3,000?!

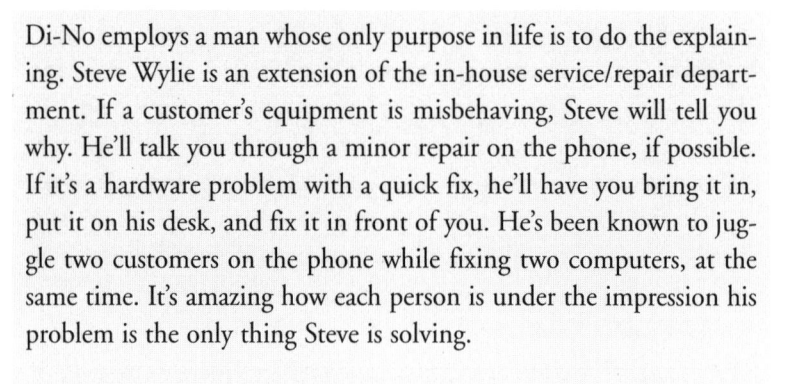

Di-No employs a man whose only purpose in life is to do the explaining. Steve Wylie is an extension of the in-house service/repair department. If a customer's equipment is misbehaving, Steve will tell you why. He'll talk you through a minor repair on the phone, if possible. If it's a hardware problem with a quick fix, he'll have you bring it in, put it on his desk, and fix it in front of you. He's been known to juggle two customers on the phone while fixing two computers, at the same time. It's amazing how each person is under the impression his problem is the only thing Steve is solving.

Thanks to such personalized service, Di-No's customers seldom shop anyplace else. Service excellence goes well beyond repair. Members of the sales staff have personal relationships with many of their customers. Like an old time grocer's, where the owners knew just what kinds of food you bought each week, these men and women are aware of the software and projects their customers are involved in.

When a new product arrives that will fit certain customers' needs, they'll call them up and tell them about it. They won't wait for customers to read about the new item in a magazine three months down the line. Their customers need this information today! Yes, the phone call may turn into a sale. The company is in business to make money, after all. But the call was motivated out of interest in their customers' success, not greed.

Of course, you can get computers cheaper at a superstore (after you've done all your own research into what makes and models, software and peripherals will best suit your needs). But what happens once you're home? Call the store for help and a salesperson will give you the manufacturer's phone number. The manufacturer will tell you the problem is with the software. The software company tells you it's the hardware. Meanwhile, you can't get your book finished and your editor keeps screaming "Deadline, deadline!"

Sal says they're lucky to break even on service – but it's the service that drives sales. Di-No's customers trust his employees, and that trust results in profits. Yet computers by themselves have little or no profit. Peripherals and software products make you the money. Even so, it takes some healthy volume to make that ship float. So, the question that begs to be asked is: Where does Sal get the money to employ a gang of specialists who all support families?

First, his sales crew receives a base salary plus commission. The harder you work, the more you make. I like that. (More on commission in Chapter Seven.) Second, Sal runs a tight ship. Although no expense is spared to ensure quality, not a dime is wasted anywhere else. Sal also boasts that his store has zero employee theft. Period. He's devised a system that keeps his employees out of harm's way. Eliminate opportunity, and theft becomes a non-issue.

He's got inventory control and cash flow down to a science, too, having tracked the company's records penny by penny (and worked it all out on his Mac). Computers are expensive, with little return, so Sal only carries what they can move immediately.

Being an oasis of help in the desert of ignorance has created an in-store climate that's half fun and half pure relief... fun for employees, relief for customers. Di-No Computers doesn't consciously compete with anyone. They just do what they do as well as they can. A new Macintosh store has opened in their neighborhood, and Apple is putting an outlet in the mall. Three superstores within spitting distance sell computers by the truckload. No one at Di-No is too concerned.

They know that boxes don't make up retail. People do. And they've got the people thing down. Sal spent the early part of his life watching his own Mom and Pop do what was right by their customers. He has replicated that experience in his own store. Customers prefer the Mom and Pop experience, and the big guys simply cannot provide it. Now that's a sweet tune indeed.

Chapter 4
Where Has All the Service Gone?

Only two things are indigenous to the United States: sales and jazz. We still do one of them well. Think about how recently you've had an unpleasant retail experience. I'll bet it was within the last 30 days, if not minutes. America invented retail, and now we do it worse than anybody else. Go to the mall. You'll find the finest employees minimum wage will allow.

They have no training, no authority to use the brains they do have, and no reason to be there other than the fact that the register cannot ring itself up. They don't know the merchandise and don't get paid enough to care to learn.

I know one musical instrument retail chain with an employment expectancy of 39 days for the sales staff. That's better than an annual turnover rate of 900 percent. How on earth am I going to get advice from someone who has such limited knowledge about what they're selling and even less incentive to care?

I'd bet the farm the president of every major retail chain knows how I feel. These folks sit in their boardrooms with platoons of butt smoochers and come up with the most righteous of ideas to increase profits and endear their customers to them. The head of a 500-store chain didn't achieve that position by not understanding how retail works. The problem is that by the time the ideas filter down to the actual people charged with selling the goods, they are unrecognizable from the original concepts.

The regional VP gives the order to the regional manager, who puts it in a pile with the 15 other new policies he has yet to implement. He then passes it along to the store managers, who put it on top of the 25 faxes and e-mails they received yesterday. Each store manager must now rely on an apathetic sales staff to pull it off. And many of them are only working there because it's easier than looking for work somewhere else.

The situation is so extreme, it's given birth to a whole new way of retailing. First, such stores offer money-back guarantees on all their goods. They have to. The odds of you buying the wrong item are great. They believe that by making returns easy, customers won't mind the inconvenience of coming back again and again. They're wrong.

Do you realize that when you give a customer her money back, it's the ultimate failure as a retailer? The very act is an admission you could not satisfy this customer on any level. A superstore gives your money back and calls it "service" – when you're actually getting a refund because service is the one thing the store could not provide.

Unfortunately, many customers don't know they have alternatives. They only shop at the superstores and the mall because Mom and Pop haven't done an adequate job of letting people know they exist.

The second characteristic of this new retail "style" is to make the store itself a salesperson. The superstores are "merchandised" in such a way that, like rats in a maze, customers are forced to walk the store in a specific pattern. Marketing experts direct you to see certain items first and others last. This "forced traffic pattern" is a brilliant concept. Supermarkets have used it for eons. Ever wonder why the milk is always in the back of a store? So you have to walk through the entire place to get to it. How many times have you gone in to buy milk and walked out with eight bags of groceries? Quite a few times, I'll bet.

As a kid in Detroit, I would visit a downtown institution called Hudson's Department Store. All the fine jewelry and pianos were on the

10th floor. That meant the people with money had to travel the entire building to get to the good stuff. I wonder how many times they stepped off the elevator at one of the lower floors "just to look around."

These techniques are not only a necessity, they work very well. Yet they're no substitute for genuine customer service. They're poor replacements at best in helping you find what you need. Remember, there's a difference between finding an item and finding the right item.

So, why can't we find service anymore? Two reasons: expense and ignorance. Please don't confuse ignorance with stupidity. Ignorance means you don't know. Stupidity means you'll never know.

■ Let's look at the first reason: expense.

Up until the end of World War II, retail was a profitable and respected profession. You went to the store, saw what you wanted, looked at the price, and bought it, if you could afford it. Pretty easy. Sure, you could shop around if you wished. But when you shopped around, you weren't looking for the same item at a different price. You were looking for the same item by a different manufacturer at a different price. In other words, you weren't looking for a "discount." It was a foregone conclusion that every store would have the same price on identical products. That's just what that item cost. If you didn't want to pay the price of Comet, you'd buy Ajax instead.

After the war, our quest for goods became outrageous. With such a demand for goods, it seemed everyone wanted to be in the supply business. And with everyone grappling for the same customer, some dork invented… the discount store. He not only introduced the buying public to a new concept, he launched the trend that ended up killing cus-

> With everyone grappling for the same customer, some dork invented… the discount store.

tomer service 50 years later. Who was this guy? We'll never know for sure, but one night some too-clever store owner woke his wife up and said, "Hey, honey, I've got a great idea! I know how we can make less money. We'll charge less. Instead of making a lot of profit, we'll make just a little!" Mrs. Dork thought he was a genius.

When the merchant across the street saw what his competitor was doing, he thought to himself: "Hey, I can make less money than that guy. I'll charge even less." A third store owner saw what they were up to and made a bold decision: "I'll show them who can charge the least. I'll go out of business. I win!"

I'm not kidding when I say discounting is like going out of business on the installment plan. You simply cannot offer customers both the best prices and the best service. It's impossible. Service is expensive. As long as you make a healthy profit, you can afford to give customers anything they ask for, regardless of how silly it seems.

Nordstrom is always an easy example when talking about exceptional service. They're famous for it. Urban legend even tells of a woman who returned a set of tires to Nordstrom – and they don't carry automotive products. But they could "afford" to make her happy. Everyone who ever shopped there paid for those tires, because they'd paid full sticker price on everything. The store makes enough money everyday to maintain the class act they have become.

You might think people would take advantage of such a store. Some do. But the reality is that 98 percent of all people are honest and just looking for their money's worth. The remaining two percent will try to do you harm. The problem is most retailers worry about protecting themselves from the two percent and turn their back on the other 98.

How many times have you walked into a store and saw a list of rules to follow if you wanted to shop there? You know the ones: "No shoes – no shirt – no service. $15 fee for returned checks. Shoplifters will be prosecuted. No refund without a receipt. Do not enter this room without a salesperson. You break it – you bought it. Screw you – go home!" Do they really think a dishonest customer will stop writing a bad check because he sees a sign? "Hey, I was going to write you a bad check but I saw your sign and decided to pay cash." The only thing those signs do is make 98 percent of your customers uncomfortable.

My wife and I went shopping for kitchen tile a while back. Walking into a "wholesale" tile store, the first thing to catch our attention was a banner hanging across the store that screamed "NO REFUNDS!" It seemed to us that the odds of buying the wrong tile at this place were so great, they had to warn us beforehand. Thanks for the tip. We left.

If you want to hang a sign that speaks to your customers, try: "Welcome! Please touch everything. Have fun while you're here. And please come back – we like you!" Customers are the only thing in the world I don't have enough of. Why on earth would I want to reprimand them like naughty children?

Now, if you're working on slim margins (i.e., discounting), you won't have the money for service – any kind of service. You can't take merchandise back *carte blanche* like the big boys and return it to the manufacturer regardless of its condition. The manufacturer will eat it rather than anger an account that does tens of millions of dollars with them. With you, they play hardball. They make you eat it because they can.

So you have to find another way to offer true service. Why not start by selling your customers the right product in the first place? Then you won't even be in a situation where the customer wants to know your policy on returns. Little profit gives you little leeway. So, you have to come up with another way to increase your margins. You'll have to reduce your overhead.

Cutting payroll is the quickest and most dramatic way to lower your overhead. Unfortunately, it's likely to cost you more in the long run. I stopped by a national camera chain outlet to get my new camera repaired a while back. A lone employee, 21 years old at most and almost in tears, was answering the phones, running the photo developing machine, waiting on customers, and receiving stock from UPS. Three impatient customers stood in front of me. I was angry – not at her, but at her company for abandoning us both. When they close that store for poor performance, the parent company will blame it on Wal-Mart.

I sometimes shop at a discount drug store that has eight checkout lines. I've never seen more than one register open at a time. But it's cheap!

The alternative, of course, is to take the official stance that your store is self-service. Self-service is a way to offer zero service and have the public accept it. Kmart is one of my self-service heroes. For the last 40 years, they've been telling me they carry the cheapest products on the planet and not to expect any service. In all that time, they've never let me down.

But it's McDonald's I credit for the end of personalized customer service in America. Before McDonald's told me to bus my own table, the thought would never have occurred to me. At first, I didn't mind. The burgers were 15 cents. For a 50-cent meal, I'll go out of my way. But now a meal with the kids is 20 bucks. And for $20 they can bus their own tables. When I go to fast food restaurants with friends, I always leave my tray behind. My friends always say, "Ed, aren't you going to clean your table?" I always reply, "They may have you working for them, but until I see an employment application, they're going to clean it up themselves."

After fast food came the gas stations. When I was growing up, you pulled into the filling station and a man in uniform and hat materialized and asked what he could do for you. The concept was that gas and oil are dirty, and you're not dressed for it. So, we'll take care of you. And besides, you're the customer – the only thing in the world we don't have enough of. Nowadays, we have people spilling gas all over their Cole Haan loafers and going home smelling like they've just cut the lawn.

The full-service pump at my local station costs 50 cents per gallon more than the self-service island. On my way to a formal event one day, I pulled into the full-service area and asked the attendant to fill it up. It was raining, I was wearing a tuxedo, and I couldn't afford to show up at this function looking like a drowned rat. I then asked the guy to check the oil and the air in the tires. For an extra 50 cents a gallon, I wanted my money's worth.

He refused! When I insisted, he said he'd check the oil but there was no way he would do anything about the tires. In fact, he actually said "they look fine to me." This gas station's corporate parent just reported a $16 billion profit! For that much money they should wash and wax my truck on every visit.

The McDonald's syndrome... We now have an entire generation of young salespeople who've never experienced any kind of service anywhere. Unless we train them well, how are they to provide something they have no first-hand knowledge of? These employees are not stupid

> We now have an entire generation of young people who've never experienced any kind of service anywhere.

or rude. They just don't know what the rest of us are expecting from them. Do you think they would even notice quality customer service if they saw it?

The other day I was driving down the freeway when my gas light went on. I was nowhere near home and unsure I could make it back to my neighborhood. I pulled off to look for a gas station. I found one, drove in, got out, and started to fill my tank. A man came out and said, "I'll take care of that for you."

I pointed to the self-service sign, thinking he'd mistaken which island I'd pulled into. He replied, "It's only self-service when I'm busy." I actually felt woozy. If this station was in my neck of the woods, I would buy gas nowhere else.

Not all self-service stores are bad. It's only the ones that advertise great service and give you none that I object to. Then there's the membership superstore. I like this place. They don't promise anything they can't deliver – and every time I need a case of ketchup, I know just where to get it. "Hey look at that! A rain barrel of mayonnaise for $67.38 – on special!" Let's face it, I don't need anybody to help me pick out a beach ball. I don't need a sweet smile in order for my credit card to be approved either. But I want one.

Discounting does have some advantages for retailers. You don't have to worry about getting the best deal on advertising (you won't be able to afford it). Payroll will be a lot less (you won't be able to hire any employees). Your wide variety of merchandise will no longer confuse customers (you won't be able to support but a few manufacturers). And if you discount long enough and deep enough, you won't have to worry about customers at all. You'll be out of business.

The good news, however, is that people don't mind paying for service. Yet most retailers seem to believe all consumers are interested in is a cheap price. It's all I see advertised. I'm not sure people respond to the word "sale" like they used to. What does it mean?

A furniture store in Las Vegas used to have "Liquidation Sale" painted on the side of its building. Every few years the owner freshened it up with new paint. We laughed every time we were in town and drove by the place. The store eventually closed – the public finally caught on.

As I said, people will gladly pay for service. You just have to be creative. Consider how one car stereo chain in Los Angeles charges for service. This company cracked a deal with a car rental agency for a daily rate of $25 for a compact roller skate with hood. They then add $25 to the price of every install job over a certain amount. When a customer gets the news that he must leave his car all day to have a new stereo system installed, the salesperson says with a smile: "Oh, do you need a car? We'll get you one at no extra charge." The customer is elated. And after all, let's be fair. Shouldn't he get a car? I mean, he paid for it. This store's customers love the extra-special treatment.

In my years of retail experience, I've learned that only one or two customers of every 10 walking into your store are shopping on price and price alone. Do not set up your business to accommodate these people! They are not the customers you want. You want to be the Disneyland of retailers: the most expensive and the most fun.

Just don't forget the other side of the sword. If you charge more, your customers had better get more in return. If you pocket all the "extra" profit, customers will perceive you as too expensive. "Too expensive" is a place where you don't get enough for your money.

Do you think people shop at the mall for the bargains? I think not. They go because malls offer many stores in a single location. Because mall stores are beautiful and, therefore, fun to shop at. Because malls are clean and safe. All of these things are worth the premium of a full-ticket sale. You want a discount? Go to the flea market. You'll find a cut-rate price on a compromise product and get to shop knee deep in second-class surroundings. Service costs money.

■ So much for expense as the first reason for today's lack of customer service. Let's turn our attention to the second reason: ignorance.

Ignorance is actually closely tied to expense when we speak about lack of customer service. The cure for ignorance is training, and training is expensive. It's not only expensive but an absolute necessity. It takes a billion things to run a store. You can't let your employees run it any old way they want. They need to know your merchandise, dress codes, company policies, and such administrative duties as how to write up sales and price stock.

Your people have so much to learn, in fact, it would take you six months to teach them. Even a superstore can't afford to pay the new guy that long without a return on investment. So they run new recruits through training like a Dodge through a car wash, hoping they'll come out clean and educated on the other end. For several weeks, the company sits them down in front of vendors who fill their heads with model numbers and statistics.

Yet in the end, product knowledge comes the same way it comes everywhere: one sale at a time. That's how I learned. The company I started with had no formal training program. They hired me based on the mirror exam: They hold a mirror to your mouth and, if it fogs, you're hired.

Most of my training came from my fellow salespeople. If you don't know, let me tell you this is not the most desirable of methods. My coworkers sold by discounting. I didn't even know I was allowed to change our prices! I assumed that if the item was marked $199, the customer had to pay $199. My first month on the job I had the highest margin in the company. After diligent training from my fellow staff members, I was able to drop my margin almost a third.

I often meet salespeople who tell me they don't need my help. They boast they've been selling for 20 years. I like to look them in the eye and say, "By now you probably know how to do it wrong perfectly."

The problem with training these days is lack of follow-through. Once the training session is over and the test passed, no one seems to pay any attention to the employee ever again. Just because you teach people how to do something doesn't mean they're doing it. Oh, they certainly learn how to write up an invoice. It's the only way to complete a sales transaction. They end up learning that action simply by doing it over and over again. And therein lies the secret to training: repetition.

While growing up, how often did you hear your parents yell, "How many times do I have to tell you?!" Apparently they hadn't hit the number yet. "I've told you a thousand times not to do that!!" I guess the number was a thousand and twelve. My point is that it's naïve to believe people retain anything just because you told them. It must be constantly reinforced.

Perhaps that's why doctors call their business a practice. The more they do it, the better they get. Doctors take more notice than salespeople when their technique fails, though. A dead patient reinforces the possibility that the technique might have been the wrong one. Yet the doctor seldom blames it on the patient: "Oh, if he wasn't so sick he wouldn't have died."

> Just because you teach people how to do something doesn't mean they're doing it.

Who is there for the salesperson? After training they're on their own. And let me tell you what I've learned from salespeople. They would rather do what's most comfortable than do the new stuff. It's not because they're bad. It's because they're human. So training must be continuous. Not just on new merchandise, but on everything that was taught the last time they were trained.

The greatest deficiency in retail training today comes in two flavors: what I call "customer care" training and plain old sales training. Good salespeople must anticipate what customers need to make them happy. You rarely find such customer care these days. Today's retail employees don't look at their jobs as missions of mercy. They don't see the customer as a human being who needs to be saved from the confusion known as shopping. They're simply not trained to be compassionate and empathetic. Consider the following example:

I went shopping for a book on telemarketing at a superstore chain, one of those places with great coffee. I arrived just as they were opening and, being one of the first customers of the day, figured I'd be back in my office in a heartbeat.

I asked the young woman behind the check-out counter where I could find a book on telemarketing. She told me to try the business section. That sounded fair. I looked on the shelves in the business section for 20 minutes with no success. Then I noticed another section labeled "Sales and Marketing." "I bet that's where I'll find it!" I thought. After looking at about a billion books, reading their covers and flipping through the pages, I hit pay dirt after 30 more minutes.

I returned to the sales counter in triumph and handed my book and credit card to the same young woman I'd spoken with earlier. As she rang up the sale, I mentioned my surprise that the store didn't have a computer in which staff members could type a word – "telemarketing," for example – and find out exactly what books are in stock and where. She looked at me with an air of innocence and said, "Oh, we have that."

I stared back in disbelief: "Do you mean to tell me you could have found this book for me when I first came in? Why did you send me wandering around the store to do a 50-minute search for something you could have gotten me in five minutes? You could have given me customer service and consciously opted not to?"

She folded her arms in disgust and said, "Will that be all, sir?" I replied, "Wait a minute. Don't cop an attitude. I have a right to be upset."

Magically, a manager appeared and asked if there was a problem. (You can always tell the manager. He's the oldest teenager.) "Yes, I have a problem," I turned to him. "Amazon.com is kicking your butt – that's my problem. If I get no service from you and no service from the Internet, I might as well buy from the Internet. I don't have to leave the house, and they'll deliver it to my front door!" The boy manager just looked at me and said, "I understand. Have a nice day." What? Have a nice day?! It's too late for that.

In fairness, I should tell you I recently returned to the same store. It killed me, but I couldn't find what I was looking for at my favorite Mom and Pop. That time I asked the clerk if she could look my subject up on the computer before I began my shelf hunt.

She not only checked the computer, but walked me over to the proper section and helped me find the very book I wanted. I asked her if the company trained her to do this or if she just had good manners and a good heart. She laughed and replied that the bookstore had just begun a new training program and this was part of it.

Here we have a perfect example of the head office knowing what needs to be done. Was the woman who made me search for my book the first time untrained, or simply unwilling? When I got my "have a nice day" walking papers, did the boy manager then teach her how the event should have gone down?

It doesn't really matter. I'm a reader. I went out of my way not to shop at that bookstore for at least a half dozen purchases after that frustrating experience. That young woman singlehandedly cost her employer several hundred dollars' worth of business.

As people like my grandparents knew, retail is not so much about boxes as it is about people. If your first concern is helping someone who needs it, the boxes will move on their own. It's hard to make employees understand this. The ones who do are special indeed. They are the people who will make your business.

The local news recently reported that a neighborhood tire store owner is scared because a Sam's Club is moving into the area. He fears that, because he can't match Sam's Club on prices, the giant will bury him.

Translation: "I've been in business for 23 years and have done nothing to cement my customers to me. I've done nothing to make them want to return to me for the years of faithful service I've given the community. My customers have no loyalty and will dump me for a couple of bucks. And besides, I have no idea how to compete on anything except price. Therefore, the superstore will put me out of business."

This man has been in retail for more than two decades – and still has no clue about the fundamentals of human behavior. I've spent a career in retail selling merchandise at full boogie when the guy down the street was discounting. I can't tell you how many times customers told me, "I know where I can get this cheaper, but I'd rather buy it from you."

As I said earlier in this chapter, at least 80 percent of your customers make their decisions to buy for reasons other than price. How many of those reasons had the tire store owner been practicing for the last two decades? Probably quite a few of them.

I'd also bet he had more loyal customers than he realized. He probably knows scores of customers by their first names. He's probably sold to three generations of the same family. People are already comfortable with him, know the kind of work he does, and are happy with the service. Of course, if he's been treating his customers like cattle (*à la* the supermarkets, for example), he is correct. He is in trouble. Price is the only way left to compete.

Independent retailers, you see, have the greatest opportunity of all time these days because most of them have forgotten how to act like the specialists they by definition are. We'll talk more about customer care in the next chapter. First, let's meet two specialist retailers who really know how to put the care in customer service.

Specialist Spotlight on... Covina Valley Schwinn

Richard Roth is a tall, blond Viking of a man, 39-years-old with his own business. He's in the same line of work his father started in when the dad was a kid. They sell bicycles. In fact, father and son each owns his own shop and sends customers to the other's store. Between the two of them, they make sure everyone in the neighborhood gets what they want.

When Richard's dad, Wes, was in high school, he started to work part time in a Schwinn store that had been around since 1934. In those early days, the bicycle was more than a viable alternative to the automobile. There was a Depression on. No one could afford a car. If you didn't ride a bike, you walked.

Bicycles were more than toys, and the bike business was a serious enterprise requiring serious attention. When Wes wanted to try out for the baseball team, the owner of the little bike shop gave him an ultimatum: "Play baseball, or work for me. You can't do both." Needing the money, Wes went to work.

All through high school and college, Wes learned the bicycle business, and in 1961 he bought the store. It was actually Richard's grandfather who saw the potential value of owning the shop. With the Baby Boom booming and the economy thriving, it seemed like a smart decision. Brother, was he ever on the money! Within a few years the store was selling 5,000 bikes annually, making it one of the largest Schwinn dealers in the country. To give you an idea of that figure's significance, Richard notes that the average bicycle store today sells just about 1,300 units a year.

Things were different in the 1960s, of course. Fewer bike manufacturers to begin with meant fewer to support. Dealers didn't have suppliers breathing down their necks for numbers. There was plenty of business for everyone.

Those manufacturers that were around practiced "select distribution." This meant that if you carried a popular brand in your store, no other store in the neighborhood would be allowed to carry it. Customers couldn't cross-shop between dealers, which guaranteed your profit margin. (Today's manufacturers practice "confined distribution" – selling their products to everyone they "con-find.")

Society was also a good deal more low-tech back in the 1960s, meaning much less competition for customers' disposable income. Rollerblades, Gameboys, skateboards, scooters, computers... unheard of! Where children were born, bicycles were sold.

One item that did come along in the 1960s, however, was the ten-speed. Long-distance riding was a reality at last. With a new breed of rider encompassing every age group, the bike business exploded.

Bikes were suddenly more expensive and more complicated. Dealers had to know more than just the length of chain a particular bike needed. The customers were now experts as well, and they wanted brand-name trick components to replace factory features.

Any time you have a boom, you'll find entrepreneurs ready to cash in on it. Brand names began to grow in numbers along with places to buy them. The traditional brands received less and less of the available pie. To keep their numbers up, manufacturers expanded distribution. Margins fell, and fewer people walked through each dealer's door, because there were more doors to walk through. Dealers began to feel they were losing their identity as specialists. Sound familiar?

Today, you can buy bikes at Toys "R" Us, Wal-Mart, sporting goods stores, drug stores, and flea markets. Unsuspecting shoppers go home with "knock-off" brands identical to the real thing at a third of its original price. The bike looks the same – therefore, in the customer's mind, it is the same. What's a girl to do? Compete where the other guys can't, of course.

First, if you've been in business for a while, let everyone know how long when you advertise. Rather than including the date your company was founded, put down how many years you've been in business. The year 1982 wasn't that long ago. "Specializing in Bicycles for 20 Years," on the other hand, makes a powerful statement.

You could also point out how many bicycles you've sold since your doors first opened. You'd be surprised how many units you've moved when you add up the years. When Wes and Richard started doing the math, their total came to more than 100,000 bikes.

Let the local superstores compete with that! What are they going to come back with... "Free slurpy with every mountain bike"? You have to establish your ground.

The next thing the Roth boys do is care about their customers' long-term needs. They interview every one. Wes and Richard need to know who the bike is for, how old the rider is, how many kids are in the family, and what kind of riding they plan to do. They don't just want to sell you one bike. They want to sell you *all* your bikes.

If you have three kids, that bike will be passed down. Dad will definitely pop the extra money for something built to last a decade rather than having to buy three similar bikes in the next few years. And did you know a quality bike holds 50 percent of its value forever? If you're not going to pass it down, sell it.

Who's going to be your advisor at the big-box store? The warehouse manager? He should. He's the one who puts the bikes together.

January is one of Wes and Richard's busiest times. They spend it reassembling the Christmas bikes bought at the superstores. Most come in with the frame backwards, brakes mis-assembled, and the front derailleur on the back wheel.

These service customers are now members of the Roth family. They will tell their friends and relatives that you can't just buy a bicycle anywhere. You have to go to Richard and Wes. Had the superstore not Frankensteined that bike, they'd have never learned that lesson. Once again we see Goliath as a partner: drawing customers into the market to find the specialist.

The older, more knowledgeable customers are aware of the big-box foibles and look for the specialist. But which one? Well, at old man Roth's store the service department occupies fully 50 percent of the building's floor space. Not only that, but the showroom and service department are barely separated. It's all practically in the same room.

When you walk in, the first thing you see is a large stock of bicycles. As you look across the sales floor, you see one of the most impressive service departments around. Technicians toil on fancy bikes, changing out parts and assembling dreams. The mega-dollar tooling machines for custom work are prominently displayed. To the serious rider this scene vouches knowledge and confidence: "Hey, these guys know what they're doing."

You'll never find that at a big-box retailer. It's not what they do. They sell big boxes. The employees don't much care what's inside them.

Another element of service at Wes and Richard's shops cannot be seen but sure is felt by this company's customers. The service there is somewhat... divine.

Richard, who originally set out to become a minister, holds a degree in theology. Between his search for a ministry and his love for the bike business, he has found balance. He works as the youth minister at his church and a bicycle expert to the secular world.

Richard deals with his customers from his heart. He truly loves the clients who patronize his store. They are people first, and customers second. This is the "warm fuzzy feeling" you always hear about but never find. Dealing with Richard gives you a sense of calm. You feel he cares. It's the way he does business, and it works for him. God knows, it'll work for you, too.

Chapter 5
All Things Being Equal, I'll Buy at the Cheapest Place

At the monster warehouse membership stores we're little more than cattle. No one there remembers who we are. It would be like expecting the ticket taker at Dodger Stadium to remember your name the next time you pass through the gate. Yet knowing a customer's name is a powerful tool. It says you're one of the family, a friend. Someone who is cared about. One's own name is the sweetest of all sounds. I've seen stores take this idea a step farther. They have their customers' photographs hanging on the wall. Believe me, once your picture is up there, you're one of the gang. And gangs hang. I think a retail industry that could benefit most from this lesson is the grocery business.

Let's consider a few all-too-common retail experiences and what you can learn from them about genuine customer care.

■ **Do you make an attempt to know your customers by name? Do you expect your employees to follow suit?**

If you have a family of four with the eating habits of average Americans, you spend about $200 a week at the supermarket. That's more than $10,000 a year. Now, I ask you, if you had a customer who spent more than 10 grand a year at your store, year after year, wouldn't you know that person's name? Brother, I'd know their kids' names, their dog's name, and their mother's maiden name. I'd know their hobbies, the sports they played, and the names of their teams. $10k a year! Every year… year after year after year!

Yet how many cashiers at the market know your name? How many of them care what it is? How many times have you been in line while the cashiers discuss their personal lives across the aisle? They couldn't pick you out of a lineup three minutes after you left the store.

I once lost my patience with one of these cashiers. "Excuse me! Would you stop talking and pay attention to me... please?" For a second I thought I was out of order. Then I looked back. Every other customer waiting to check out was giving me a thumb's up – lined up with crowbars, brass knuckles, and boxing gloves just like in the movie *Airplane*. Ever get the feeling you're just in these employees' way? And they have the nerve to wear little signs attached to their aprons (aren't they cute?) with the message: "My name is Sally. Ignoring you since 1988."

You see, superstores have forgotten a very important retail lesson. People have a choice. They can shop anyplace they like. Why should I shop with them? If that little sign read: "My name is Sally. What's yours?" within six months all those cashiers would know all of their regular customers' names. It would become the *Cheers* of supermarkets. But that's never going to happen in the grocery business.

In fact, a recent news story reported we'll have self-service "checkout" counters one day soon. Eventually they'll just e-mail my groceries directly to my hard drive. Then we won't need any social skills at all. Our children won't be able to speak to each other. Bank robbers will use store-bought greeting cards that read: "Congratulations on your robbery. May this day be a special one. Please give me the money. I have a gun, so don't get cuter than this card."

■ **Do you treat your customers with the politeness you expect from your friends, your family, your children?**

Last year a small grocery store opened in my neighborhood, directly across the freeway from the supermarket I usually shop at. The owners have done an excellent job of emulating the big guys. Nobody says, "Welcome! How do you like our store?" Instead, they ignore you, treat you like a criminal with every personal check, and display no manners. The first time I shopped there I used my Visa debit card to pay for about $60 worth of groceries. I use the card continuously, have never bounced a check, and have $2,000-worth of overdraft protection for emergencies. The store's computer system was brand new. It denied my card. In front of seven other customers in line, the cashier yelled, "Your card's no good. Do you have another one?"

Embarrassed to be called a deadbeat in front of all those people, I quietly asked her to try again. "Nope, they turned you down again," she yelled. "What do you want to do?" I told her to put my groceries back where I got them and left.

You cannot expect people to have the same definition of manners that you do. That cashier had not been trained. She was hired because she had been a cashier at a local supermarket. I know this because I recognized her. The owner probably thought she was a plug-in employee since the big guys had "trained" her. They had. And she acted exactly in her new job the way she had at the old one. Yet in the confines of the small grocer's, her coldness was much more dramatic than at the large supermarket. No one had ever told her to be considerate with customers, to use her head and the manners her parents taught her. (Oops, maybe those *were* the manners her parents taught her.)

■ **Is your store an interesting or fun place to shop? How would you define its atmosphere?**

The owner of this new grocery store was missing another important factor. The place is clean, sterile even. The atmosphere is so cold it's no fun to be in. The next time you visit a major grocery store, check out the decor. Pretty, color-themed graphics and creative seasonal displays deck the walls. The store just feels good. Listen – you'll hear music. Music makes people happy, and happy people buy more. Ten years ago grocery stores only played Muzak. Now you hear upbeat rock and roll. I hear people singing as they shop all the time. Yet the music is not simply for your enjoyment. Grocery store owners aren't trying to entertain you; they want you to buy more. Walking into this new market by my house, you can't tell if you've come in the front or the back. The whole place looks like a stockroom, and it's dead silent. Shopping there simply feels awkward.

I must admit this doesn't surprise me. The same man owns the liquor store in this little strip mall, too. Having done well with the liquor place, he decided to run the grocery store the same way. If it worked for the first store, why not the second? What this man doesn't realize is that at the liquor store he's basically selling drugs. When people are looking to get high and/or ingest a little nicotine, they'll buy it out of someone's trunk if they have to. But if I'm going to do my family shopping, I want something different. Buying a bottle of Jack Daniels for Saturday night takes me about three minutes. Grocery shopping takes me an hour or so, and I do it twice a week.

So, being Mr. Bigshot and assuming everyone wants my advice, I paid the owner a visit. I tried to explain what makes a shopping experience special to consumers. I pointed out that he's missing several key ingredients, that the place needs some redecoration to add an element of fun. I suggested that his employees make an effort to learn his customers' names. I emphasized what a tremendous opportunity he has.

As I spoke, he just looked at me with an expression that said, "Are you actually from this planet? I've never had a customer speak to me like this in my life!" When I finished, he smiled and pointed to the door.

■ **Do you ever take your customers for granted?**

Believing you have a right to your customers is a retail disease. Grocery stores offer plenty of great examples, but I don't think any industry or market is immune. I once needed a model of a sailing ship from the time of Cleopatra for a charitable project. Rather than visiting a Toys "R" Us, I headed to a local hobby shop near my house.

The lady behind the counter was working on something that I was apparently interrupting. I stood in front of her until she finally looked up and asked, in a flat tone, "What do you want?" I described the model. "Nobody makes one," she said, turning back to her work. I suggested that if I wanted one, someone else in the world might want such a model too, so there must be one on the market somewhere. "If there is, it'll probably cost $300," was her response. "Fine – let's find it!" I said. Since the price hadn't scared me away, I guess she figured she would. "I can't help you," came her final reply.

This woman didn't know me from Bill Gates. I could have been a model ship hobbyist looking for the specialty store of my dreams. But helping me was too much trouble. I returned home, found the very ship I wanted on the Internet, and bought it straight from the manufacturer for $75 plus shipping.

■ **Do you *always* put your customers first?**

One time at my local video store, I couldn't find a soul to wait on me at the check-out counter. When a lone employee appeared, I asked what had happened to everyone. "They're all working" came the reply. Yes, they were... tagging merchandise and putting away stock. We can't let customers interfere with our jobs now, can we?

> We can't let customers interfere with our jobs now, can we?

So much for customer-care training. Let's take a look at sales training. The best merchandise selection, savviest promotions, and the most polite sales team in the world won't help you take the leap from surviving to thriving if your employees don't really know how to sell. Yet most people think sales is something you do when you don't know how to do anything else. Judging by the people who wait on me, I can see why the public feels that way. In fact, I used to feel that way myself.

For years I was a nightclub entertainer. I played guitar, told jokes, and worked all the time. I had no other job for more than 15 years. I was a professional. I could do something few others could do. I offered my talent, and people paid me for it. I made a living and raised a family. I was very proud of that. I came from a family of professionals. One uncle was an engineer, another an attorney, and my father was a manufacturer. Although my family did not look upon my chosen profession as the true and righteous way, they couldn't deny I made a good living and got to sleep until 10:00 every morning.

I refer to the places I worked in as "nightclubs," because my mom wouldn't let me work in bars. But bars they were. And after spending five nights a week for a decade and a half in bars, I couldn't face another drunk. I had to find a "real" job. So, what do you do when you don't know how to do anything else? Easy. You become a salesperson. You certainly don't have to know anything to do that.

In the beginning I was embarrassed. Like most people, I viewed salespeople as the slime of the earth. My mother used to yell at me all the time, "You want to end up a salesman like your Uncle Frank? Go to college and learn something important." Now I have to tell you my Uncle Frank always drove a brand new Caddie and vacationed in the Bahamas every year. He made more money than my uncle the attorney. I was embarrassed being a salesperson just the same. I had turned my back on my true "profession" and was working in some hi-fi store and waiting for something to happen. I hated my job, I hated the customers, and I hated my lot in life.

Now, a guy named Alan worked in my store. Alan was our number one salesman. I recall Alan selling a turntable (a device used to play vinyl records) and taking it to the counter to write up the sale. He looked at his customer and asked, "Need any record cleaner?" "No." "How about a stylus cleaner?" "No." "How 'bout some speaker stands?" "No." "Then how about a tape deck?" "No!" "Then how about some tires for your car?" "No! No! No! No!"

After the man left, I asked Alan why he was badgering the customer. He said he wasn't badgering his customer; he was just asking him if he wanted anything else. "If I didn't ask, I would be saying no for the customer," Alan explained. "Customers know how to say no all by themselves. They don't need any help from me." Yeah, right. I hated Alan, too.

Then one day, as I stood behind the counter (the perfect place to meet everyone else's customers), a man came in to buy a videotape. I resented him for coming in and bothering me, and I resented him for wanting something for which we received no commission. (In those days videotape cost $20 and were bought one at a time.) I know this is going to be hard to believe, but I was rude to him.

Out of the corner of my eye I could see Alan watching me to see if I would try to add-on to the sale. What was I going to do, ask the guy if he wanted a turntable to go along with his videotape? So, just to annoy Alan to the max (I couldn't have cared less about the customer), I looked the man in the face and asked, "Would you like a videotape

> "If I didn't ask, I would be saying no for the customer."

recorder to go along with your videotape?" The phrase "jerk-face" was implied. The startled customer looked back at me, then said with a sneer, "No! I already own a videotape recorder or I wouldn't be buying a videotape!" The word "jerk-face" was implied back. I looked over at Alan with a triumphant glare.

Alan motioned with his hands that I should continue. As I looked down to collect my thoughts, I spied a video camera on the floor. I asked the customer if his machine was portable. "Yes," he replied impatiently, "I can take it anywhere I want and play it there!" "Do you have a video camera so you can take pictures of the kids and send the tapes to grandma?" I asked.

The next words out of that man's mouth changed my life. Not just my attitude, not just my mind – but my entire life. The customer looked up at me and said, "Do you take American Express?"

I had made a $2,200 add-on to a $20 sale!

That's when I realized sales is not something you do when you don't know how to do anything else. You have to know how to "do" sales, too. You can learn the techniques, things to say to make a sale happen on purpose rather than by accident. It's possible to be a professional at this, too. From that day forward, I followed Alan around the store like a puppy, begging him to "teach me more, teach me more." He taught me more. To this day I still sit in on every seminar I can. I know there's something I don't know, and that drives me crazy.

What kinds of formal training do you offer your staff? Books, videotapes… anything? Lack of material available on the market is not an excuse. There's tons of stuff out there – not just my own products (although I'd definitely begin with them), but many books and materials designed to assist salespeople on the floor. Ask yourself, "Who taught you how to sell?" If the answer is "no one," you have an excellent opportunity. Good management is like a game of follow the leader. Study the same training materials as your salespeople and practice them together. Don't leave your staff susceptible to failure – or at best, to succeed purely by accident.

Many people don't know Benedict Arnold was a famous Revolutionary War general before becoming a famous traitor. His fame grew from the fact that, unlike other generals, Arnold actually led the charge into battle. When the troops saw their boss putting his life on the line while asking them to do the same, he inspired them to follow. Lead the charge in your store by learning how to improve your sales skills along with your employees.

Remember, there's little reason to return to a superstore except for price. Give me a smile, a clean store, good knowledgeable advice, and genuine interest in my needs as a consumer – and I'll be back forever. So will your other customers.

The tire store owner we met at the end of Chapter Four had little faith in what he had built over the years. All things being equal, I'll buy at the cheapest place. As a retailer, it is up to you to be as unequal as you can. The only threat to your business is your own apathy. If you are a specialist, and act as a specialist, you will not lose your customers. And the most powerful weapon in the specialist's arsenal is... knowledge. Get some. Make your staff as unequal as possible compared to those superstore giants down the street.

Specialist Spotlight on... L&W Appliance

L&W Appliance is 70 miles from St. Louis, 250 miles from Chicago, and across the street from Middle America. Frank Wildhaber, owner of the two-store company, has been in business for 27 years. He's successful, dedicated, and believes the secret to his success is a willingness to try the untried and never take business for granted. "If you don't help your customer," he says, "someone else will."

Frank began life as an air conditioning contractor. Since his hometown of Litchfield, Illinois, has only about 3,000 houses, it wasn't tough to get to know an awful lot of people. His customers thought he was pretty cool, too. When they had appliances that needed repair, they asked Frank for help. It wasn't really his business, but he had a knack for electronics and liked helping people out. If he couldn't fix something, he'd help the customer replace it.

As time went by, Frank found himself replacing lots of irons, mixers, and refrigerators. So he decided he might as well turn his business into an appliance store – a store that just so happened to have an HVAC (heating, ventilation, and air conditioning) contractor's license. Frank became the guy in town to see!

Not unlike a thousand other retailers, Frank is excited about what he sells. His work is more than just a business – it's his whole life. And he's more than just involved on a day-to-day basis – he's committed. Do you know the difference? Consider a plate of bacon and eggs. The chicken was involved; the pig was committed. It's all or nothing.

Frank's enthusiasm is not lost on his employees. They've been with him for years, and he keeps them excited by involving them in almost every aspect of the business. He holds weekly sales meetings and invites manufacturers to his stores on a regular basis to keep the crew abreast of new products and technology. Just the other day, GE and Maytag reps were in his stores conducting sales training.

Yes, Frank does everything right. He had even joined a buying group to ensure he receives the best pricing possible on his products. He sent his son to college for a degree in HVAC and then hired him to run the company's air conditioning division. Unfortunately, being smart about business doesn't guarantee growth, and growth was the one thing Frank did not have enough of.

Although his original store always enjoyed an annual increase in sales, the second store never experienced the same kind of steady success. Both featured the same merchandise and were run basically the same way – and a town of 8,000 people could certainly support two stores. So what was going on?

Frank, being Frank, decided to make a few changes. He'd heard of an organization called Best Brands Plus and decided to join. These folks offered independent retailers much more than just great buying power. Dedicated to their members' success, they coached them on training, advertising, merchandising, and expansion.

Although most retailers can use at least a little help in all of these areas, it was the group's thoughts on expansion that most caught Frank's attention. They pointed out that a storefront was available opposite the area's new Wal-Mart – and that 19,000 cars fill that retail giant's parking lot every day.

That's at least 19,000 people who would have to come from all the little towns in the surrounding area. Towns whose residents have never heard of Frank or L&W Appliance. Frank realized the answer to his sales slump was right in front of him. In fact, he was kind of embarrassed he hadn't realized this sooner. A friend who owns a Maytag dealership had moved his store right across the street from a Circuit City. And even though Circuit City no longer sells white goods, Frank's friend is doing great. The exposure to all those shoppers has doubled his business.

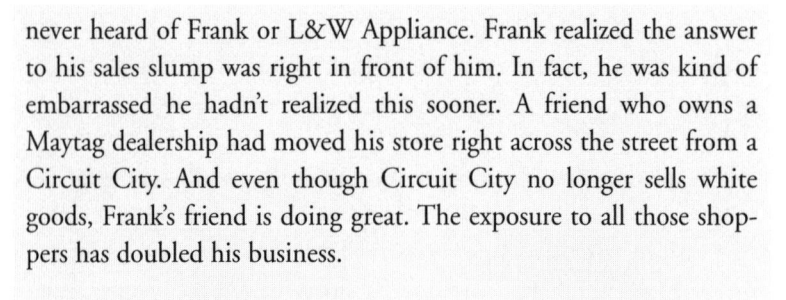

So Frank moved his second store right across the street from Wal-Mart. Had it not been for the advice of the folks at Best Brands Plus, he would never have made the move. The new location is the same size as the old one – about 7,500 square feet – but each square foot is earning him much more money.

All too often, people are afraid to ask for help. They confuse running out of new ideas with being stupid. Buying groups are terrific – and, as Frank learned, the right buying group can change your life.

Think about how many people in the world you haven't met. Just about all of them. Now think about how much you haven't learned. Just about everything there is to know. The only thing new in the world is the history we haven't uncovered. Successful specialists are not smarter than you, nor do they have any more talent. All they have is more information.

So join a group, read a book... and get yourself some new ideas for succeeding as an independent retailer. With a few fresh ideas and some old-fashioned customer service, Frank has been able to make his new location as unequal as possible in the shadow of one of the largest retail giants around.

Chapter 6
Reviving Your Personal Trade

You can't buy the *best deal* in advertising. I'm talking about the word-of-mouth buzz spread as happy customers talk to their friends, family, and folks they meet on the street. Word-of-mouth advertising is the secret of all secrets in retail. It's a direct result of the relationships you have with customers – relationships that make shopping with you so much fun, relationships I call personal trade. And personal trade is the one thing superstores cannot pull off.

Why not? Simply because their employees aren't around long enough to see customers a second time. Not only that, but they didn't read this book. They don't know they're supposed to have personal relationships with their customers – that the shopping experience should consist of more than just dollar bills and credit card slips changing hands.

Many larger companies try to create the illusion of personal trade. Ever notice who those "greeters" at the superstores actually greet though? People their own age or families with kids. If you're 30 years old and have a tattoo, they pretend you're invisible. As I've said before: Management has no control over what happens on a sales floor. A savvy executive decrees that every customer must be greeted but has no control over who actually receives that friendly "hello."

Heck, half the time I can't get salespeople to notice me when I'm smack in front of them. In an electronics superstore the other day I stood in front of three employees chatting away. One guy finally noticed me and asked if he could help. "Where can I find the blank CDs?" I asked. He pointed me in the right direction and went back to talking.

Do you think this chain approves of that kind of behavior? Of course not. And where was the manager? Probably in a back office buried in paperwork his regional manager sent over that week. He'd love to be back on the sales floor, acting like the effective boss he was promoted to be. But paperwork takes precedence over customers.

I don't care if the UPS man is waiting or the building is on fire, if there's a single customer in your store, that person is your number one priority! Too often I see customers' time taken for granted – as if these stores have an endless supply of shoppers with hours of free time on their hands. What a great opportunity this gives Mom and Pop!

Think back about what made you successful at the start of your career. I bet you had many a sleepless night the week before your first store opened. Not from fear or worry, but sheer excitement. You fantasized how the carpet would look… which manufacturers would give you more credit… whether you've arranged the displays to best effect around the store….

Not once did how much money you were going to make cross your mind. Your thoughts were more along the lines of: "How much can I afford to lose before they take the house?!"

It was that concern, foresight, and passion that made your company a success to begin with. And each customer who walked into your store was precious. In fact, customers were the only thing in life you couldn't have enough of. That's why you took a special interest in each one of them.

"How can I help you?" was not an empty line. You knew everything your store had in stock, and customers sensed you sincerely wanted to help. Your personal trade grew out of such hands-on interest in the people who chose to shop with you. Reviving your personal trade is a sure-fire way to make your store as unequal as possible compared to the superstores. First though, let's consider how *not* to get personal with your customers.

My wife and I went shopping for a coffee table at a furniture chain a while back – one of those stores where you walk 100 yards through a warehouse to get to the showroom. Upon our arrival, all we could see through the glass showroom doors about 25 yards away were what appeared to be a bunch of suits and ties. As we approached, the bunch vibrated. When we hit the glass doors, a person with hand outstretched broke free from the pack: "So, how can I help you?" she exclaimed.

This woman walked directly behind us while we cruised the 60,000-square-foot showroom. It dawned on me that my wife and I hadn't said a word to each other since walking in the store, thanks to our uninvited eavesdropping shadow. She not only made zero attempt to speak to us but gave the unmistakable impression she was there to keep my wife from stuffing a sofa under her dress and taking off with it. I had to stop myself from telling her to jump down a manhole. If we wanted to shop with her, I would have called her from the house before we left. Finally, in a voice loud enough for the people at the front door to hear, I said to my wife: "Gosh honey, you were fantastic last night. I had to turn on the light to make sure it was you!" Our shadow vaporized into thin air.

Now, I knew exactly what was going on. We call it the "up system." You all lie in wait at the front door. The first customer is Sally's, the second Don's, and so forth. Whoever is "up" gets the customer. If you have eight salespeople on the floor, you might wait an hour for your turn. You only get to talk to eight customers a day, so when you get one, don't let that poor person go. You won't get another chance at a commissioned sale for 60 minutes. Handcuff 'em until they buy something or leave.

There's nothing wrong with the "up system." The problem is that managers rarely train employees how to work the system without making customers uncomfortable. This woman should have simply let us go.

> Managers rarely train employees how to work the system without making customers uncomfortable.

She should have acknowledged to her colleagues that she was on the case and left us alone for a few minutes. The store was so large she could have casually met up with us at any number of locations, smiling and offering a simple hello as she passed. Her opening line might then have been a question completely unrelated to business – something to identify herself as a human being rather than a salesperson tracking game.

Had she approached us in such a manner, we could hardly be anything but responsive. "I really like your dress. Where did you get it?" she might've asked my wife (even if she'd been thinking "you could hide a sofa under that thing"). In the brief conversation that would have ensued, she would begin to establish her footing on a personal level.

Only then should she have asked what brought us into the store. I assure you we would have told this "seemingly interested person" that we were looking for a coffee table. She could have shared our excitement in owning a new piece of furniture. She would have begun to develop her personal trade. Not having been taught any better, she took the low road – and we went home without the table.

When you've revived your own personal trade and taught your staff members to do the same, you've effectively woven your store into the fabric of your community. After all, whether you're talking coffee tables or carpentry tools, people like to shop where they're known – if not by name, at least where they're recognized by the staff.

Don't just wait for people to walk through your doors to develop such community ties though. If you sell sporting goods, sponsor the local Little League team. If you own a hobby shop, sponsor an outdoor crafts event for kids. The best of the big guys do this kind of thing all the time. Let everyone in the area know who you are. Don't keep trying to lure them in with low prices. You'll never win at that game. Lure them in with good news – about you and about your community!

Let's take this idea one step further… If you'd like a sense of community in your store, try moving into one. Rather than finding a storefront on a street with slightly less traffic than the freeway, find a cute little downtown area. Small-town downtowns are the retro rage. People feel like they're shopping Disneyland's Main Street without the big mouse. Each store occupies its own cute little building with a distinct personality. The business owners meet everyone in the neighborhood. And if their first experiences at your store are enjoyable, they'll be back.

When I was a rep, I once walked into a retail store where I'd been doing business for years. The fellow at the front counter told me the boss had told him he wasn't seeing anyone today – especially not sales reps. "Tell him it's me," I said. "I don't think it'll do any good," the guy replied. "I've tried with a couple of other salesmen and he was mad at me." I asked him to try anyway. The man came back with a smile on his face: "I don't believe it. He'll see you. Go on in."

As I entered I pulled the boss' leg a little and pointed out he wasn't seeing any reps that day. "Ed, I'll always see you. You're good news," he replied. "You always tell me how good life is, not how far behind I am on my sales commitment." He saw me that day because of the relationship we'd developed over the years, a relationship based not on business, but on friendship – two men who wake up with bad breath, gotta pee, fight traffic to get to work, and have kids who drive us crazy.

You can find lots of people to sell you stuff. I'd rather do business with friends. Fostering these kinds of relationships with your customers will truly set you miles ahead of the superstore "competition."

Specialist Spotlight on... Borgman's Jewelers

Chain stores like Borgman's Jewelers[1] are unique in their ability to take on the face of an independent. Each individual location is capable of developing its own "personality" based on the staff and their community. Usually located in a mall, they generally sell mid-level quality items at wonderful margins. They are the perfect place for a young man to buy an engagement ring for his sweetie.

The top salesperson at one Borgman's outlet couldn't be less stereotypical. Bess Steinberg was a housewife for most of her life. Her affluent husband bought her things that let the world know he was doing very well. And the things he bought were made of gold.

After 42 years of marriage, Bess had decided her husband was a mistake. Her top priority after their divorce was not to find a new man, but a job. Yet she'd done "nothing" but be a housewife and mother for the previous four decades and had no idea what she might be qualified to do. A friend suggested sales, since she has a wonderful personality and a terrific outlook on life.

Bess decided she'd try her hand working in a jewelry store. She figured, why not spend the day surrounded by the things she loves. Besides, Fort Knox wasn't hiring. Although fear that her utter lack of sales experience would work against her in the interview, it didn't. The store was so short-handed, Godzilla would have landed the gig.

Bess felt justifiably out of place her first day on the job. "What am I supposed to say to customers?" she asked, and was told only "Just be yourself." Well, being a mom is pretty much "being myself," Bess thought – and I know how to do that better than anything!

---

[1] The names in this story have been changed.

Her first customers were a young couple, the same age as her own children, looking for an engagement ring. "Aren't they sweet," she thought. "I hope he won't go overboard. These kids need lots of stuff to start their life. I'll make sure they don't make a mistake."

She asked the young man what he did for a living. They teach you in sales training that this is called a "qualifying question." You might think Bess was a natural born salesperson for asking it. In reality, she was trying to find out if this young man had any business getting married. It had nothing to do with what he could afford. After a brief interview, she decided the marriage could go forward. Then she presented the merchandise.

When the couple picked the ring, Bess recalled how she had once been given a set of earrings that perfectly matched her wedding band. She remembered how much fun they were to wear. She thought these kids should have the same amount of fun, so she found a pair of diamond earrings to match the engagement ring. The blushing bride-to-be fell in love for the second time in her life. In fact, she said that if Bess had a diamond wedding band to match, it would make a complete set. Guess what? Bess did. It was her first sale – and the store's biggest ticket of the day.

The rings needed sizing, so the couple made an appointment to come back in a few days. It just so happened that Bess was doing some baking for her family the night before their return. She thought that nice young pair would enjoy some of her homemade biscotti. When they came in to pick up their purchase the next day, she gave them a little touch of home to take with them. You would think she'd given them a car. They were so appreciative they decided to buy their jewelry from her for the rest of their lives – and they have.

Bess has worked at Borgman's for 11 years now. With only two other salespeople on staff, she writes 60 percent of the business. And that's not counting the sales she gives her two coworkers. Bess has a decade's worth of customers who stop by just to say hello, then linger over coffee and her homemade goodies. She sells them their anniversary gifts and stuff for their kids.

She's developed an intimacy with her customers that goes beyond their appreciation of her as a retail employee. They consider her a family member who works in a jewelry store. Bess not only sends birthday cards to her customers, but to their kids as well.

How does she find the time? As at all retail outlets, Bess has plenty of down time. She could stand there and wait for someone to come in. Instead, she writes notes and goes through old invoices looking for customers who need a new watch to go with their banana bread.

On payday, her coworkers just shake their heads in wonderment. At this point in her newfound career Bess has so much "personal trade" she only has to work a 40-hour week to make a very comfortable living. The difference between her and the other guys is that she works all 60 minutes in each of those hours.

Bess is 76 years old and ready to retire. Her boss refuses to let her go. More vacation time… want to visit your grandchildren at the drop of a hat? Whatever Bess wants, Bess gets. After she closed the deal on a $58,000 diamond ring (at a mall!), the owner of her company called to congratulate her. "How did you do it?" he wanted to know. Bess answered with two words: "Walnut clusters."

Chapter 7
Selling the Good Stuff

The superstores have made their names as "the place" for selection and bargains. Yet their selection is not always that good. They offer a variety of items within a particular price range, but nothing above that range. If they do show a higher priced item, they probably carry only a single unit. Since they don't sell much merchandise in the higher price categories, they don't need to stock a variety of high-end products.

Superstores don't sell the "good stuff" because the good stuff needs a salesperson to explain the value of owning it. Without seeing the value in a product, the price will always be expensive.

If I could get you a Rolls Royce for the price of a top-of-the-line Lexus, would you consider that a bargain? Of course you would! Would the car be cheap? No. A top-of-the-line Lexus will cost you close to $70,000. At regular price, a Rolls would cost you about $150,000. So a Rolls at 70 grand is less than half-price. Seen in that light, $70,000 is cheap!

If I walked into a clothing store, however, and saw two blue pin-striped suits side by side – one marked $249.95 and the other $600 – how would I know the difference without a salesperson? I need what the superstore cannot provide: an expert. Someone to teach me that the $600 suit is a "super 120" (120 weaves per square inch) and is made of wool that feels and wears like silk. It hangs straight and won't wrinkle – an important factor if I travel.

To me, the cheaper suit *appeared* just fine. Had someone pointed out the value of the super 120, however, thereby raising the drool quotient, I might buy that one instead. I often wonder how many people don't own a top-of-the-line item for the simple reason that no one showed it to them. How can I buy something I don't know exists?

By the way, which of those two suits had the most profit in it? The super 120. If the store had it on sale for $500, which suit had the most profit in it? The super 120. Do you think the dealer would ever sell the $249.95 suit at $100 off? Only as an alternative to throwing it away. There's not enough profit in that suit at full price as it is. Why discount away what's left?

I once worked for a manufacturer who came up with a device that cost us $7 to make. We were going to sell it for $20. Wow, what a profit! Unfortunately, we'd have to sell 10,000 of them just to cover the cost of setting up the manufacturing. It wasn't worth it. It's not any different in retail. Your salespeople are better off selling a $1,000 item and making 10 percent than selling a $50 item and making 40 percent. It's the same amount of work. You're not in a contest to see how many items you can sell. You're in a contest to see how much money you can make. You can't "make it up in volume" if there is no volume. The superstore has the volume – you don't. So, you'd better make the difference up at the register.

One of the ways to play the price versus value game is in the way you mark your products. Commodity stores (books, groceries, shoes, et cetera) are often the exceptions, but in many specialist retail categories you can make legitimate arguments over whether or not to mark the prices on merchandise. Some argue that price tags make a store look more professional. The big-box retailers mark all their prices, allowing customers to comparison shop.

Others claim that price tags allow customers to shop without the assistance of a salesperson – something they definitely don't want. Remember, it's the specialist salesperson who will explain the value of products available at different price levels and ensure that the customer purchases the right item the first time. Yet many customers don't trust a store with unmarked merchandise. They think there's a hidden price that's a better deal than the one they're about to get.

So, what's a specialist to do?

In my experience, entry-level items are the fastest moving merchandise in a store. Since few salespeople in retail truly know how to sell, they let price sell for them. My customers want inexpensive products, these poorly trained folks claim. They're wrong, of course. Their customers want a bargain. The two are not the same.

Do a little research into your competition. What do they charge for the most popular items you both carry? What's featured in their latest round of advertising or in-store promotions? Those items are the ones customers will most likely cross-shop at your store. Forget about their price for a $3,000 computer, $5,000 sub-zero refrigerator, or the 3.2-liter engine on a TORO riding lawnmower. Find out what they've marked the iMac, the Kenmore, and the mower that's not going to cut the lawn at Versailles – the "action range" items. Then you mark those items only. You never mark the good stuff.

Why? Customers who've been shopping around for a specific item immediately see you offer competitive prices. This gives you credibility. And if yours is an industry with more male customers than female, it's worth remembering that men typically buy at the last place they shop rather than return to the store where they started. If you can grab their interest, there's a good chance they'll stay.

Yet if a customer has no preconceived ideas about what to buy, the "empty tag" gives you the chance to pitch the better quality, more expensive, more profitable item. The empty tag itself begs questions.

> It's worth remembering that men typically buy at the last place they shop.

Let's say you're 40 years old, make a good living, and have decided that riding a bike several hours a week will get you another 40 years. You visit a few big-box retailers, stop by the discount department stores, and check out the classifieds.

Unfortunately, all your shopping around really hasn't helped. You've seen so many makes and models you have no clue which bike would be best for you (although you do have an idea of what the bikes you've seen should cost). More importantly, you've only been shopping one kind of retail outlet: the non-specialty discounter. They don't normally carry the "trick" stuff – in fact, most high-end manufacturers won't even sell to those guys.

You walk at long last into an independent bike shop with a $300-400 price tattooed on your brain. The first bike you see is marked $1,200. "These prices are outrageous!" you think. You have no idea this model's quality is five times that of the bikes you saw elsewhere. Sure, you can afford the $1,200, but you have no intention of being taken advantage of. You go home with a $350 model that's good enough, but…

Were the bike not marked, you might have asked a member of the sales staff to describe its features. He gives you the pitch, and you fall in love. Then he tells you the price, and you flip. You tell him you were looking for something in the $400 range. He apologizes and shows you a model in that category. You hate it. The quality simply cannot compare to the first bike. You go home with the $1,200 ride and enjoy it for years to come.

Have you ever noticed jewelry stores have all the prices in code? It forces the salesperson to take each piece out of the cabinet and put it in the customer's hands. It offers the customer the opportunity to fall in love.

"Doesn't that look nice on you?" Had the customer realized that the watch was tagged at $1,100, she may have never asked to see it at all.

Tagging only the most popular products on the market won't work if you haven't trained your sales staff on the mechanics of the process. Too many retailers out there focus on boosting their ad presence to draw in new customers – customers they can't sell to once they're there.

Think about it… if you stocked all the merchandise your customers wanted, at the exact prices they were looking for, guess what you wouldn't need? Salespeople, because you would really be little more than a giant vending machine. But you don't know what customers want at the prices they're willing to pay. Finding out that information is the salesperson's job. And if your salespeople don't know how to do their jobs, you're in for some frustrating days.

Before we move on, let me add that no amount of training will create a professional sales staff unless they're on commission. If you don't have a commission plan now, the transition can be rough. People who've never worked on commission worry they can't make it. They have little confidence in their abilities. You must assure your people that, at the very least, they'll make what they're earning now.

The specifics of implementing an effective commission plan that all your workers are behind 100 percent are not important here.[2] The reason for implementing a commission plan *is*. The right commission plan will ensure your customers receive from you what they cannot get at the superstore: personalized service.

---

[2] Don't worry. I'll be discussing how to determine commission rates, ways to get your staff to sign on to this new pay structure, and related management details in book two of the *Good News About Retailing* series.

As we discussed in Chapter Four, people will pay for service. Anytime I see a sign announcing "Our Salespeople Are Not On Commission," I translate those words to "No Service Offered Here." Store owners advertise that their staff members are not on commission because they think consumers believe commissioned salespeople are dishonest, pushy, and rude, willing to do anything to make the sale, and always tricking customers into buying things they really don't want.

None of this is true. To begin with, nobody can sell you something you don't want. Period. Second, customers could care less how you get paid. Rudeness comes from a lack of training and manners, not from your company's compensation structure. BLOCKBUSTER is a perfect example. Here is a storeful of kids making minimum wage and loving life.

I've shopped several of their locations and had the same experience each place. I walk in the door and the cashier, already handling several customers in line, looks at me over her shoulder and says, "Welcome to BLOCKBUSTER." The next employee to cross my path does the same. I have to believe they've been trained to do this because it happens each time I go there. I'm starting to think these kids like me!

Proper training makes the difference between a pushy salesperson and an assertive one. Asking five times in a row "Are you sure you don't want to check out our summer swimwear? It's on sale…" is pushy. Asking – and taking no for an answer each time – whether the customer requires a jacket for his new slacks, a dress shirt, a tie or belt, or free pressing of a jacket he already has at home is not being pushy. It's making sure the customer goes home with everything he needs.

And a well-trained employee can identify exactly what customers are likely to need based on what they ask for initially: a camera bag for the new digital camera, an extra-long printer cable for the computer, batteries for the new travel alarm, and socks for the shoes. When the salesperson works on commission, these items are less likely to slip through the cracks. And the poor guy with an interview tomorrow doesn't get home to find his old dress shoes need resoling and his belt is two sizes too small.

Providing proper training and expecting good manners of your staff is only half of the commission issue, however. Your employees must have the opportunity to make a real living. If the net result of a new commission plan means they go from earning $8.25 to $8.75 an hour, you will not see the results you want. Walk into one of the electronics superstores. Those people are on commission, but the pay rate is so low they have no incentive to help anyone but themselves. Create an atmosphere where an employee can support a family, and you'll have an employee for life.

I've written this book both for retail owners and for managers who wish to take ownership of their stores – in other words, the leaders at all levels who want to thrive by helping their companies do more than just survive. And the great thing about commission plans is that *everyone* has the opportunity to take ownership in your store. Well-trained commissioned salespeople take better care of customers because they are *their* customers, not just the store's. They've taken ownership of the process – and the results. You've made it in their best interest to sell the good stuff while treating customers to superior service.

Specialist Spotlight on... Logan's Hardware

Covina, California, is one of those great little cities the fruit industry gave rise to in the late 1880s. Whether by chance or design, the downtown area has kept the same architecture and attitude for more than a hundred years. The city still looks pretty much like the black-and-whites hanging in the local restaurants. Fifteen miles east of Los Angeles, Covina exudes the charm of an old movie. Downtown Covina is bustling. Although every major superstore seems to have an outlet within a couple of miles, the shopkeepers still enjoy brisk traffic. The people who live in Covina find most everything they need downtown. Besides, it's a fun place to shop.

Just after eight o'clock on a cool April morning, 75-year-old Don Matheson sat at his computer in Logan's Hardware filling an Internet order for 35 washboards. It seems it's difficult to find washboards these days. Logan's has been selling them since 1919. Before moving to its current address, the store was named Logan's Whip and Buggy Supply. And although Don is not the original owner, he's very proud of the fact his business license is Number 18 in the city of Covina.

Logan's Hardware carries some 20,000 SKUs in about 2,500 square feet of space. You need to turn sideways to move down the aisles. It doesn't take many customers to pack the joint at many specialist retailers. At Logan's, the number is five. At the hardware superstore up the road, the number is 500.

Don knows a lot about his business, having begun work in a hardware store as a teenager. After college he became a sales rep for a hardware manufacturer and spent the first part of his career helping store owners. Having been in retail himself, he sold them only what they could move. He was not interested in short-term relationships. He was also a gadget freak. He used the stuff he sold. And the enthusiasm that ensued made him a great salesman. In fact, Logan's Hardware was one of his accounts. He had been a rep for 18 years when the store came up for sale. Don knew both sides of the business, wholesale and retail, inside and out. The timing felt right, so he bought the place.

Don is an old-fashioned kind of guy. Born in the 1920s, he was brought up appreciating the Mom and Pop mentality. When he bought Logan's, it had already been a local institution for 60 years. Don determined not to modernize the way it did business. With its tin ceiling and wood-planked floors, the place felt warm and safe. And with the building boom of the 1950s and 60s over, his was the only hardware store left in town.

Ten years after the purchase, the first of the superstores arrived, Builder's Emporium. Because Logan's serviced the local community with their day-to-day hardware needs, Builder's didn't affect him dramatically. He never catered to the contractor trade. Lumberyards and plumbing supply houses felt the tremor more than he did. And besides, the local giant was still too far away. People didn't want to travel three miles to score a screwdriver. Within the next five years though, The Home Depot, Home Base, and Lowe's moved into the area. Logan's finally felt the pinch. Although Don's longtime customers were loyal, Logan's didn't experience its usual growth. Newcomers shopped at the superstores because they were so visible.

The first thing Don noticed about the big boys was the way they marketed themselves. They began by advertising unbelievably low prices on power tools – prices the little guy simply cannot match. Their cost on these goods was lower than Don's. They tagged that product so close to that lowered cost, the resulting retail price made you feel you'd died and gone to homeowner's heaven. Customers were so excited about the bargain they got on an expensive piece of equipment, they didn't notice everything else in the place was 15 percent higher than the local guy. There's never been a free lunch, after all.

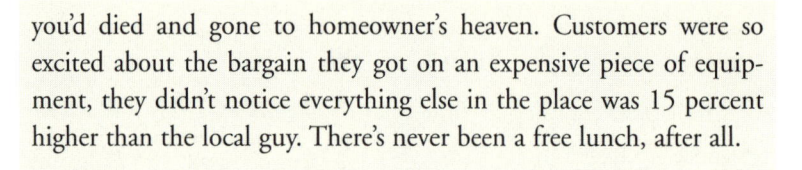

Having been a rep, Don knew the way the superstore operated. They worked on the 80/20 principle. That meant 80 percent of their stock had to be the fastest moving items they sold. They couldn't afford to stock items the average consumer only needed a few times in their lives. You could certainly buy a cheap hot water heater at Builder's, but not a hot water heater pressure-control valve. The superstore infrastructure wouldn't allow them to carry it. If they only stocked a few pieces of a single item, nobody would be able to find them.

Don decided to become the store that carries the stuff you can't find anywhere else. His slogan is "Try Us First." If you need one bolt, why should you have to buy a box of 50? He's done such a great job exploiting this niche market that The Home Depot down the street sends him scads of customers every day. And because his product knowledge is so keen, he sells these people everything they need to finish their project – not just what they came in for. Sound familiar?

Oh... Did I mention the harmonica? Don's been playing the harmonica for 50 years. Walk into the store on a slow day, and you'll hear music drifting in from the backroom. The only thing missing at Logan's is a pot-bellied stove. Every week during the summer, locals come to a farmers market in the park across the street. Don sits out front, sporting a work shirt and three-inch-wide suspenders, and entertains the crowds as they walk by. Don is a very successful retailer. That's why there's one musical style he never plays: the blues.

Chapter 8
Learning to Lead!

As the owner or top manager, you've always taken special care of your customers. Yet the more successful you are, the less time you have to spend doing just that. How do you teach your employees to treat customers the same way? My wife's been trying to teach me to be sensitive for years. She says I'm doing better and hasn't fired me yet. Were we not married, though, how long would she put up with me? It seems it was years before she actually told me what she wanted. I heard a lot of: "Well, if you don't know, I'm not going to tell you." Now that she tells me, it's much easier on both of us.

It's no different with you and your staff. If you want to beat the big boys at the game of retail, you must become the neighborhood store the customer would rather shop at. And you do that through personal relationships – not just with your customers, as we learned in the previous two chapters, but with your employees.

To start, you need a clear definition of what you want your people to do before you can expect them to do it. You must explain the big picture, so your employees understand *what* you are trying to achieve and *why*. This is called leadership. And by definition, leadership is proactive.

Leaders don't sit around complaining about problems. They try to solve them. I once told my boss about a problem our company was having. He asked me for the solution. When I told him I didn't even have a suggestion, he told me to leave. His stance was that you only have a right to complain if you have an idea about what needs to be done. You don't even need to offer the right solution. But, if you offer nothing, you're just making things worse by worrying others.

Being a leader is certainly not easy. (Just keep in mind that it's not nearly as hard for you as it is for a manager at a superstore. Those poor people are so busy doing other things they don't have the time to take care of their own staff.) Why is leadership difficult? Because real leaders don't wait for someone else to take the initiative. If you ever hear someone say, "Somebody ought to do something about X, Y, or Z," that person is not a leader, natural-born or otherwise. Natural-born leaders (if there is such a thing) have a clear vision about what needs to be done. If leaders need help, they'll admit that fact and recruit assistance.

Unfortunately, when it comes to leadership, it's easy to fool yourself. I think back to my first days as a store manager many years ago. I had set ideas about how I wanted my staff to behave. You know, how to offer my version of customer service. At my first store meeting, I lectured those lucky employees with my insights into the consumer psyche. The sales staff liked me, so I assumed they would follow my lead.

Several months into my tenure, the outfit I worked for sent all store employees to a management workshop. The company owner theorized that if he trained the entire staff as managers, everyone on the team would be able to anticipate what must be done in the store.

My staff sat around a table and prepared to describe, one by one, our store's customer service policies. I spoke first, reciting my famous speech. The trainer nodded in approval and turned to the next person. This is really going to make me look good, I thought smugly, since I've instilled the entire staff with my inspired dogma.

As it turned out, not a single member of my crew actually did any of the things I thought he was doing. Each one had his own agenda and style. Here I thought I was a leader of men. It turned out I was just a nice guy who had all the keys to the store.

This realization was one of the hardest pills I've ever had to swallow. I was embarrassed and hurt, but I had learned a great lesson. Just because you tell someone something doesn't mean they've heard you. And just because your title is "boss" doesn't mean you're effective.

Apparently leadership was something I was going to have to learn. If the crew likes you, they won't kill you. It doesn't go much beyond that. Learning to lead sure didn't come naturally. I had to work at it. I took classes. I read books. I studied.

And I learned that leaders don't need a sparkling personality, an MBA, or the build of a fashion model. They need simply a clear vision about what needs to be done. A leader will consider the various options for reaching a particular goal – and then take the path of least resistance. The weak get their feathers ruffled and the strong say "Yes ma'am!" You can't take the position that it's not your job. It is.

A good leader will inspire others to become leaders as well. They lead by example. They teach and nurture. They encourage. As a result, they build a motivated staff by making sure their employees are successful at their jobs – and teach them how to make others successful. They're called team builders.

Not everyone is comfortable in the roll of leader, of course. Some wind up with the job by default. The other person is gone, and you're the only one left. Some do it for the money, and some do it for the prestige. Real leaders do it so they can accomplish a particular goal. For them, being in charge is the easiest way to maintain their sanity.

Nothing is wrong with being a follower. Not everyone in the world wants to be the one responsible. But as a follower, the minute you ask

> Apparently leadership was something I was going to have to learn.

someone to do something so you can finish your own work, you've just given yourself a promotion. Enjoy it – you've earned it.

Taking the reins of leadership is only half the battle. Successful retailers must motivate their people to follow. You want your employees to be the customer service team people cannot find anyplace else. If you're to differentiate your store from the giant retailers, this is one of the major pieces of the puzzle: motivated staff members, employees who will do what needs to be done – not just because it means their jobs, but because they know it's the right thing to do. When they say good morning to a customer, you can hear the sincere intent behind the words. You need a crew whose behavior at work is "on purpose."

When it comes to motivating your staff, the myths are as numerous as the cure for hiccups. No magic pill exists. In fact, you cannot really motivate your employees to do anything. People motivate themselves.

Now, don't confuse this statement with the newspaper ads you've seen. You know, the ones that read "Self-motivated salespeople wanted." Translation: You're not going to get any help from your new employer. If you're going to work here, you're on your own. Nobody wants that.

Nurture your staff, train them in the skills needed to shine as specialists, and they'll rise to the occasion. Treat them like fools, and they'll rise to that occasion as well.

Hardly a person in the world enjoys failing everyday. If your new salesperson makes no sales, he's unlikely to be the most motivated member of your staff. If your assistant manager can't seem to get the hang of monthly inventory reports, he won't be having much fun either. They're likely to be late every day, look disheveled, or have negative attitudes about their jobs. Let's face it, what do they have to be excited about? They're failing. You can threaten them, write them up, or offer a bonus. None of those things will improve their skills.

When it comes to raising the morale of the staff, I used to think if I was nice to employees it raised their spirit. I thought if I took the entire office out for dinner, they'd like their jobs better. I was wrong.

There's only one way to raise morale: *raise production*. I don't mean you should request a raise in productivity. I mean, help make it happen. When I was on the sales floor and had a great sales day, I couldn't wait to get to work the next day. I was a winner! My morale couldn't get any higher. Production equals morale.

So there's only one cure for that salesperson or assistant manager with the blues – some sales for the former, a successful project for the latter. Teach these potentially valuable team members exactly what needs to be done and why. When they do their jobs correctly, stroke them until they faint. You'll have employees with a terrific attitude.

Now, apply this concept on a store-wide scale. Don't wait for your employees to get to the point where they're walking around with long faces because they can't seem to do anything right. Offer them the training and nurturing they need from the outset. Remember, a leader has a vision of what needs to be done – training is how the leader communicates that vision to the rest of the group.

Let's consider an easy example, applicable to retailers of every shape and size: the constant hassle of keeping your store clean. Where people work, trash and clutter will follow. As a store manager, I used to get so tired of employees telling me that they're in sales or accounting, not maintenance. These folks had absolutely no desire to help. Yet most small companies can't afford an outside cleaning crew. Finally, I sat everyone down at our weekly store meeting and explained the *financial* benefits of keeping the store clean.

First, it separates us from the competition. It makes us special. And in the case of the superstore, it makes us equal. They're already clean – really clean. Second, it's easier to shop in a clean store. A "straightened" store is less confusing to the eye. It makes the atmosphere less frantic and has a calming effect on the customers. We want them to feel comfortable. We clean the store so we can sell more.

Once the crew understood my reasoning, it was easier to get them to clean the store. They understood the purpose behind my request, so they were more willing to get it done. By tying sales directly to our store's condition, I was no longer just a bossy boss, but a leader showing the way to greater profits for us all. I still had to prompt them, of course, but they did it without the usual grumbling. And if someone balked, I pointed out they were costing the company business.

If you lead your people by eliminating such roadblocks of ignorance, you'll have an incredibly willing staff and a stress-free job. Lack of motivation for them to do the right thing – to follow your vision of how to succeed – will never be a problem again.

Specialist Spotlight on... Allied Model Trains

Joshua Lionel Cowan loved to invent things. At the turn of the 20th century, when a new invention seemed to appear every 20 minutes, he invented the electric flowerpot. Push a button, and a light would come on to illuminate the flower. The idea was a terrible failure – it had something to do with watering the plant.

Not to be discouraged by minor details, Cowan looked for new ways to harness electricity for the betterment of mankind. Inspiration struck one day in 1900 as he gazed into a jewelry store window. How neat it would be to have a little train pulling a miniature flatcar around the display window, he thought – each car loaded with bracelets or rings to dazzle passers-by. What a great idea!

Well, he was right – almost. Customers filled the jewelry store, clamoring to buy. But they didn't want jewelry. They wanted one of those little trains. *Voilà*, the Lionel Train company was born.

Electric trains have captured the imaginations of children in every country and generation since. Between 1946 and 1956 (the industry's largest growth period) America went nuts for trains. It wasn't actually the kids who went nuts, of course. It was their parents. The kids were just an excuse. Now that dad had a better job, he could afford the toy he always wanted.

Allen Drucker had such a dad. When Allen was about four, his father brought home a train set. Not a Lionel, but an American Flyer. They were every bit the quality of Lionel, but somewhat smaller and built to scale. It was beautiful. And at $40, it was no toy.

Poor Allen was forbidden to touch it. His father said it was too fragile for little boys. So fragile, in fact, that pop only brought it out at

Christmastime. Around and around the tree it went, year after year. When Allen was eight, the American Flyer finally became his.

As Allen grew, so did his love for model trains. He became a collector. And like any Jones, Casey or otherwise, he had to sell some of his inventory to support his railroad habit. Allen became well known across the nation as a trader in new and rare model railroads.

In 1975, he sold his house, his car, and a portion of his private collection to raise enough money to buy a broken down little model train store in West Los Angeles. He renamed it Allied Model Trains.

Allen was in stationmaster heaven. His knack for selling and love for the merchandise made him a success. But Allen had an even greater vision – one he couldn't make good on until 1988 when, once again, he hocked his life to build his dream store in nearby Culver City. A store that had it all.

Unless you're a model train enthusiast, you can't really comprehend what having it all means. Allied Model Trains carries some (hold on...) 100,000 SKUs. On my visit, I saw a really small bag with little air horns in it. These horns go on little trucks that wait at the little blinking railroad crossing.

Allen is quick to point out he carries these horns in four different sizes. You see, model trains aren't all the same size. You've got big ones, smaller ones, little ones, and teeny-tiny ones.

The train and track of a model set are defined as a specific "gauge" or scale – that is, a percentage of actual lifesize measurements referred to by a letter (Z scale train, for example, can literally fit in the palm of your hand). Each gauge has its own array of people, houses, pets and livestock, trees and plants, and countless other accessories that are sized proportionally.

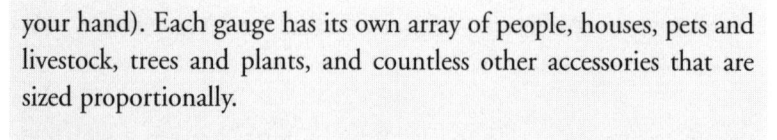

So, how do customers know what to buy? Enter Allen's 12 salespeople. Each is an expert in a particular gauge of railroad and/or accessory line. If you haven't guessed by now, the money is in the accessories, not the trains.

Back in the 1940s and '50s, model trains were a 40-point item. These days the profit margins run between 18 and 30 percent. Combine that with traders and hobbyists willing to make little profit on a deal, and it's easy to see the money is in the add-ons.

So, with an overhead the size of Texas, how does Allen draw folks into his store? With the building itself.

The dream store Allen built in 1988 is a replica of Los Angeles' historic Union Station. What better place to buy a train than the train station? The lighting sets the mood, and the merchandising whets the appetite. Two enormous displays of complete little mountain towns bring out the child in every adult walking into that store. From the dance hall floozy hanging out in front of the saloon to the dog giving the eye to a fire hydrant, the detail is absolutely amazing. Each small locomotive pulls eight to ten magnificent cars on multilevel tracks, along the walls, between the walls, through the mountains, and into other rooms.

From floor to ceiling, model trains in every size and configuration imaginable fill the walls. Allied sells quality sets starting at $120, and the price tags go up from there. The first engine I spotted when I walked through the door was priced at more than $5,000. My friends, this is a specialty store!

The place is immaculate. Allen points out he only needs 10 salespeople. The extra two keep the store clean and pick up the slack when it gets busy. On Saturdays you can barely get into the building. While waiting for the place to open, I watched an employee inside a display window washing it down. How dirty could it have gotten since yesterday? Staff members immediately remove any product they spot in a box with a crumpled corner. Only when a new box arrives from the manufacturer is that item repacked and returned to its shelf. Think this is going a bit far? Allen drives a Rolls Royce, so you tell me.

This little specialty store is world famous. Framed magazine articles hang everywhere. One feature titled "Sinatra's Train Store" reveals that Allied was the only place Ol' Blue Eyes liked to shop. The April 1994 *Los Angeles Magazine* – with an article headlined "300 Reasons Not to Leave LA" – lists Allied as reason number 14.

Allen explains that he wanted to build a store that would leave a lasting impression on any visitor – one that would compel customers to tell everyone they know about this incredible place. The result is not just a supreme example of specialty retailing but a local landmark.

Okay, the guy works hard, has a one-track mind, and does very well. But is there anything extra special about this man and his business? There is indeed. *Allied Model Trains and similar specialty stores have actually forced the superstores out of the model railroad business.*

In the old days, if you were in the market for an electric train you went to a department store. They always had one in the window at

Christmastime. The toy department sold extra track, a few different cars, and a handful of little buildings. Department stores eventually gave up on their toy departments altogether and, as the different gauge railroads became increasingly popular, the superstores just did not know what to carry. No one on staff could talk trains... or discuss the accuracy of a scale model with a rivet-counting enthusiast.

Their employees are basically clerks who sell boxes, so customers ended up home staring at mismatched products. The proportions were all wrong. You had Lilliputians interacting with the Jolly Green Giant. The tracks were too large or too small for your train.

Besides, what superstore would be inclined to stock an air horn not much bigger than the head of a pin... in four different sizes, no less?

By the very nature of their specialty, the model railroad industry has made it impossible for Goliath to play their game. Allen and specialist retailers like him have been instrumental in creating the rules that keep the big guys out. So the next time you're in Southern California, visit his store. You can fly into LAX, drive down the 405, or, better yet... take the train.

Chapter 9
There's Nothing Casual About Business

So what else can you do to make your store unequal? Outstanding, personalized customer service is definitely the most dramatic change you can make in your operation. Small details make a huge difference, too. Things the superstores already do well that you are just as capable of doing just as well.

Most malls and superstores are beautiful. It's the number one reason people like to shop at them. The richest and the poorest of shoppers all get to have a first-class experience. It costs you little or nothing to excel in this arena, too. Paint, carpet, and displays are all cheap when compared to the return on investment. Are customers having fun the moment they arrive at your store? Does the place look good? Does it smell good? You can do it!

■ We've already mentioned the first thing you can do just as well as the big guys: Clean up your store! Think about how you feel walking into a Disney Store. I don't care how old you are, you have fun just standing there. At the one in the mall near my house they have a zillion televisions against the back wall playing *Snow White*. And everywhere you turn you see a smiling face. You know how to smile.… So compete! You have a vacuum cleaner.… Use it!

You know how you clean up your house when you're expecting company? You want to make your guests think you really live that way. Well, brother, you have company coming into your store everyday. They're called customers. And if you'll get your house in order for your friends, why not do it for the people who make you a living?

I bet you have little idea what your store looks like anymore. You're suffering from what is known as "store blindness." You've been there so long you no longer see the junk piled up behind the counter or the cracked glass in the display cabinet. And while dust-covered shelves may be just the look you're going for in an antique store, the rest of us can get along without it. You need a stranger to come in and give you an evaluation of your store. Someone to see things with a different eye.

You may not realize it, but a messy store makes people nervous. The superstores and malls have set the standard in this regard. They have full-time crews that do nothing but keep them in tip-top shape. You don't. You must do it yourself or rely on staff members. Remember, you have to make all things equal before you can become unequal.

■ My second easy-to-implement suggestion is to enhance visibility. Flood your place with light. Brightness makes sales. Take a look around your store and see how many bulbs are out. Don't forget, when you paint a sign on your window it blocks out the light. It's no fun shopping in a dingy store. Then put everything in your store parallel and perpendicular to everything else. You know, "straighten things up."

Start with an exercise right at your desk. Without removing or stacking a thing, put everything on the desk parallel and perpendicular to everything else on the desk. That includes paper clips and the trash. You'll notice how much nicer it looks even though there's still the same amount of junk present.

You and your staff must make a continuous effort to keep your store straight, if not clean. When I found one of my stores a mess, I would check the numbers before speaking with any of the crew. If the numbers were high, it meant business was so good that they didn't have time to keep things in order. A busy store is a messy one. But if business was slow and the store was unkempt, there was no excuse. The manager was simply not doing his job.

■ My third easy-to-remember idea is… Don't forget to get dressed before you go to work! And put rules *in writing* so every member of your staff does the same. The superstores sure have this one covered.

So many retailers have the attitude that "Oh, we're very casual around here." Well, let me tell you there's nothing casual about business. Business is the most serious thing you can do. People make instant decisions about the quality of your store and the knowledge of your employees based solely on their personal appearance. That people judge by appearances may not be fair, but it's certainly true.

I remember my first day at the old hi-fi shop. Almost everybody on the staff wore jeans, a T-shirt, and sneakers. Not knowing any better, I donned jeans, sneakers, and… a shirt and tie. All day long customers were asking me if I was the manager. The very fact that I had a piece of cloth hanging around my neck somehow made me in charge. I think you could wear a swimsuit with a tie and people would still think you're the manager. But it did impress upon me something I already knew: You can't tell the players without the uniforms.

Are your people in uniform? Think about a "sport sneaker" place where all employees dress like referees. Or a national auto parts store where everyone is playing "pit stop mechanic." Go to a jewelry store and you'll see the staff dressed like they're on their way to a Bar Mitzvah. What does *your* staff wear?

If you don't take appearance seriously and institute some kind of dress code, you cannot take exception to the worker who shows up in a tutu. My buddy Dave visited a gift shop in south Florida where the staff was barefoot and wore cut-off shorts and tank tops. They did indeed have a dress code. Nudity was out!

> That people judge by appearances may not be fair, but it's certainly true.

Believe me when I tell you that "dressed up" means something completely different to me than it does to Generation Y. And it's not just the clothing. People take personal hygiene for granted. How many times have you been waited on by someone with body odor that would melt a tank? Or breath that could wilt a redwood?

I try to be open-minded. I look back at hippie photos of myself from the 1960s and think, "No wonder the police beat the crap out of us." I know piercing and tattoos are popular today. I try not to be too judgmental, but I do feel uncomfortable being waited on by an illustrated pincushion. I bet some of your customers do, too.

The key is just to think about who your customers are and who you would like them to be. Then, dress up accordingly. As I walked into a client's store once, one of the salespeople corralled me. He wanted me to give him a sales tip – one that would give him "the edge." I told him to go home and shave. "No, really," he said. "Give me one." I told him I just had. He replied that I "don't know the kind of customers who come in here. They're just kids." They seldom get any older clientele, he added. I told him they probably never would.

Some people will never get it. If he walked into work at a superstore without having shaved for two days, his boss would send him home. (If the manager was actually out on the sales floor, rather than stuck in an office catching up on a week's worth of papers and wondering why business is so slow.) Not shaving shows disrespect for your customers. This idea may be old school, but why dress for just a portion of the public?

You want to stand up to the retail giants? Start by doing the things the superstores already do right.

Specialist Spotlight on... Insane Stereo

Years ago, I was a sales rep for an exclusive line of car stereo products. Every dealer in town wanted to sell my brand. But we offered the line to only a select few. The manufacturer had stiff rules. A retailer must fit a particular profile even to be considered. Being a high-end shop didn't automatically qualify you to become one of our dealers.

One afternoon we received a call from Bobby Chow, owner of a place called Insane Stereo Liquidators.[3] Bobby wanted to become a dealer and carry our line. The word "liquidator" in his store's name killed any chance he had. Far from suggesting the salon-type store that typified our dealers, the word implied he was getting rid of stuff nobody wanted. Completely the wrong image for our brand.

Now, Bobby wasn't actually a liquidator. He just used the word to lure customers with the promise of a bargain. (There was an ounce of truth in his store name, of course. I don't know a single store owner who wouldn't like to liquidate his inventory every day. The name was misleading, nonetheless.)

Well, it was my job to go down and meet the man, hear his story, and turn him down. Besides, good salesmanship teaches that today's loser may be tomorrow's winner. You should know everyone in your territory. The next day, off I went.

I knew I was at the right place when I saw "Insane Stereo Liquidators" emblazoned in paint on the side of a building. A roof-top sign screamed the same name in lights. When I stepped inside, I found an interior scene that was a direct reflection of the name itself. A short man in glasses and an old Nike t-shirt stood behind the counter. He

---

[3] The names in this story have been changed.

was making an $8 sale to a young man dressed about the same. The store itself was – how you say? – a pit. Pale yellowy-white walls suggested someone had hosed them down and let the dirty water do its thing. The torn industrial carpet no longer looked industrious. It was beyond dirty. It needed to be condemned.

A total of seven or eight stereo systems were scattered across five displays designed to hold 70. The walls sported posters affixed with tape and staples, their corners peeling back, dirty from dust getting caught on the sticky tape.

The installers were working in a parking lot behind the store. Several miles of extension cord waited on the ground for the next rains. I couldn't tell if the guy was coming in or going out of business!

Bobby himself was a nice man with a spectacular smile and friendly manner. He sincerely wanted to do business with me. In fact, he felt that without my line he couldn't make it in this business.

That news sent up another red flag in my mind. I wanted dealers who were going to make it regardless. If your entire future is dependent on a single source, what would happen if that flow of product stopped? Back orders are a way of life. What happens if you're on credit hold? What are you going to sell? You need a variety of lines for a variety of reasons. If you need me to survive, you need a better business plan.

Turning someone down is never comfortable. I didn't know how to tell Bobby his place was a dump. So, in the true spirit of American business, I blamed it on someone else. I told him I didn't have the power to sign him up. This was true: Only my regional manager could make the decision after a personal visit.

I knew if I took my regional manager to see this place, though, the dealer would not only get turned down, but I would have a size 11 shoe inserted into my body. I gave Bobby my regional's name and told him the man was so busy, he might not get to Bobby for months. He thanked me, shook my hand, and I was on my way.

About a week later I got a call from my regional manager, wanting to know why some guy named Bobby was calling 10 times a day. I told him the story. He told me to return to the man's store and do my job!

The next day I did just that. I explained to Bobby that his store did not fit the profile. "What do you mean 'profile'?" he asked. I couldn't find the words. I wanted to be fair and polite, professional and sensitive. "Your store looks like s---," I said. "If I bring my regional manager down here, I'll never hear the end of it."

He asked me what he'd have to do to make his store more presentable. I said the first thing was to change the name. Our company would never sell to a "liquidator." Next, he'd have to paint the place and put up a ceiling, replace the carpet and have his posters framed. He should combine all the stereo systems into a single display and deep six the others. That way, the displays wouldn't suggest he was out of everything he carried.

Lastly, I said, he'd have to find a better place to install equipment than an open-air parking lot – someplace permanent. Bobby said he'd looked into an industrial canopy permanently attached to the building. Cost: $3,000 – a lot of money. I told him that would be fine.

"You're asking me to spend $20,000!" he said. I told him probably so. "So, if I spend this money, you'll give me the line?" Bobby asked.

I told him that if he fixed up his place, I'd bring my boss to see him. It was still my boss' decision. "Well, what happens if I spend the money and he turns me down?" Bobby continued. I told him he'd have to settle for doubling his business.

About two months later, Bobby gave me a call. He said he'd done everything I asked and was ready for inspection. I was skeptical. I felt as if my son had just told me he cleaned his room and now wanted to go out. I told him I would stop by for a visit as soon as I could. A few days later I was in the area and swung by.

The first thing I noticed was the absence of the roof sign and the word "liquidator" from the freshly painted side of the building. Stepping inside, I was shocked. Customers literally packed the place. I couldn't see the improvements for the crowd.

Bobby came bouncing over to me like pogo stick man. I've never seen so many teeth in my life. "How do you like it?" he beamed.

I told him I loved it. He'd done everything I suggested, and the place looked great. His installers were working on four cars under the brand-new exterior canopy. The man had doubled his business!

"Now will you bring your boss down to see me?" he asked. "You betcha!" I said. It wasn't long before Bobby was on board as a dealer. He had to hire more salespeople and installers.

That was 20 years ago.... I stopped by his place recently, and the man is still doing gangbuster business. Car stereo may be an informal industry, but Bobby Chow learned just in time there's absolutely nothing casual about business.

Chapter 10
Getting the Word Out

Now that you've got your stores in shape and your employees looking and acting like specialists, how do you let all those potential customers out there know where to find you? How do you compete with those retail giants in your industry whose advertising budgets are the size of Ohio?

If possible, open a store in one of their parking lots – or right across the street like Frank of L&W Appliance did. The giants spend millions of dollars every month bringing customers into the marketplace. And as you've learned by now, they are not competing with the independent specialist. When it comes to advertising, the likes of Borders, Guitar Center, and The Home Depot are your partners. They reach much more of the buying public than your puny ad budget ever could.

And when those folks walk out of a superstore without making a purchase, do they know you might carry the very item they're looking for? Do they know where you are? Do they even know you exist?

The first thing you need is a big, big sign. The right sign is the single most effective investment you can make in retail. Just think about how many times you've actually had the address of a store and still couldn't find the place. Yes, I know your landlord said he'd put up a sign for you. But anything you get for free is worth about the same.

Some years ago when I was running a large retail chain, we hired some marketing students from a local college to find out where our customers come from. They stood at the front door of each store on a particular Saturday and surveyed the customers walking in and out.

What we learned astounded us. The majority of the people shopping our stores were word-of-mouth or repeat customers. The second largest group consisted of "drive-by" customers – people who'd driven by our stores every day, seen our sign over and over again, and logged us in their memories. When they saw our ads in the newspaper, they made the connection: "Hey, I drive by those guys every day." The smallest group of customers came from the Yellow Pages.

Getting this information was like hitting the jackpot. We'd been spending $60,000 a year on ads in the Yellow Pages, and it wasn't bringing in enough customers to blow our noses. So, we canceled those directory ads the following year and put the 60 grand into new signs for our strategic stores. Traffic increased at every single one.

When considering the design of your new sign, don't forget to tell people what you sell. That may sound obvious, but it's not. A business in my neighborhood announces its name with a beautifully lettered, blue and white sign sporting a huge anchor and announcing "The Captain's Corner." But what kind of establishment is it? Well, it must have something to do with the ocean… a tropical fish store, boating supplies? The name by itself explains nothing. It turns out to be a seafood restaurant. Yet no potential customer can tell that driving down the street at 45 miles an hour looking straight ahead.

Leave your ego at home and tell people what you do. I once increased a client's business by suggesting he hang a banner reading "Car Stereo" on the front of his building. For the next two weeks customers wanting to know how long he'd been there flooded the store. The answer: 15 years. "Gee, I've been driving right by and never noticed," they said. A sign worked for the Little Rascals. It'll work for you.

Let's see how independent retailers can effectively take advantage of the other marketing opportunities out there:

■ **Newspapers:** Independent specialists can compete in the newspaper, but you must know how, and you must be committed. Your ad must appear in the same place week after week. Eventually, when customers need what you sell, they'll mutter to themselves, "I see someone selling washboards in the paper all the time. Where are they?"

Advertising is all about repetition. As the sales rep of every publication that I advertise my own business in has told me, a potential customer must see your ad a minimum of five times before you can make the sale. A third-page square ad run six times in a row is much more effective than a full-page ad run once. In fact, any single-run advertisement is about as pointless as pitching mutual funds to an 11-year-old.

Besides, you can't afford a full-page ad unless you're in the *Pinkney Michigan Gazette*. The major metropolitan newspapers cost between $50,000 and $100,000. Yes, a day! Some company spent 50 grand for an ad I'm going to wrap my garbage in. If the paper goes to five million people, it just may be worth it. However, it's a moot point since most independent retailers don't have 50 grand just sitting around.

There are two great places to be seen in the paper: The men's section and the women's section. Certain things are just men stuff. Tires, for example. Or having your hair replaced. You need tires? You need hair? Look in the "men's section" of the paper. You know the one: It's more commonly known as the sports section. Every newspaper calls the "women's section" something different. It's the "lifestyle"-type section where you find family features, fashion and health information, advice columns, the daily horoscope. Yes, I know I'm stereotyping here, but as they say, the race doesn't always go to the fastest, and the fight doesn't always go to the strongest, but that's the way to bet. It's also the way to do newspaper advertising.

> A potential customer must see your ad a minimum of five times before you can make the sale.

■ **Television:** If you could actually afford a TV campaign like the big boys, it would put you out of business. After the first week you'd have so many customers you couldn't possibly handle them all. They'd have no place to park and no one to wait on them. After the second week a crowd would storm your building, torches in hand – like the windmill scene in an old Frankenstein movie. Cable advertising, though, can work well for independents. Even in many urban areas, cable is both affordable and effective. Since it reaches fewer viewers, you won't be faced with an unmanageable onslaught of customers.

A word of advice: Spend the extra bucks and have an agency shoot the ad on film rather than cutting corners with a home movie camera. And again, don't let your ego get in the way. Leave no doubt in the viewer's mind who you are and what you do. Repeat your name, address, and what you sell about a million times. Stay away from price. If you choose to go head to head on price with the superstores, you will lose. Stick to the things the giant retailers can't compete with you on – how many decades you've been in business, that your employees offer expert product knowledge, that Mom and Pop still work there, that your selection of specialty items beats anything at larger retailers.

■ **Radio:** If you choose to advertise on the radio, you want three things to come through: your name, your location, and what you sell. It's much more important to do this on radio than on television. On TV, potential customers can see your merchandise. Shiny sparkling things draw their attention. Think about how you can almost smell the food in a restaurant ad when you see it all dressed up on the screen.

On radio you have no visuals. If you're not giving that message every heartbeat, you're not getting your money's worth. Radio's kind of funny. I know retailers who do well with radio ads, and others who don't. Use an advertising agency that specializes in radio. Listen to some of their ads. Get a tape and listen to it in the car. If the sample ads get your attention and you don't have to rewind to get the message, that agency is probably the one to go with.

■ **Special Promotions:** The superstores base their special promotions around discounted merchandise with a theme: Presidents' Day Sales, Back to School Sales, White Sales. To promote these events, they simply run pages and pages of ads touting the lowered prices in local newspapers and barrage TV audiences with ads. They do this for hundreds of stores at a time, nationwide, and for the most part their sales crews are completely uninvolved. The sales staff needs no training or additional information about what's going on in the company. Someone higher up the chain of command has made sure each store has enough of the advertised merchandise and that the registers are reprogrammed with the proper pricing.

The superstores chuck out a ton of extra invoices as a result of these special promotions. Yet once again, the only thing the customer is getting is a good price on a specific item. If that's all you have to offer your customers, why should they return until you have another sale?

The specialist, on the other hand, is capable of doing something the customer will remember. Something that makes them want to come back to you just for the enjoyment of coming back – a promotion they will look forward to year after year.

Remember Tom from The Fret House? Well, his greatest retail triumph would have to be his promotional advertising "campaign." It began by accident. About 30 years ago Tom held a hootenanny at the store to celebrate opening day. For those of you who don't eat corn, a hootenanny is a folk music jam session. Every player in the area joined in, and they had so much fun they decided to hold it on a regular basis. They built a venue in the basement and started holding concerts – and this promotion is still working three decades later.

The first Saturday night of each month is "open mike" night at The Fret House. Anyone who wants to play gets 10 minutes or three songs, whichever comes first. Who are these players? If you guessed Tom's customers (and their friends), you're right. They can get on a stage, with a real audience, and be the star they bought their guitar to become.

The other Saturdays, Tom features professional acts from all over the country. He sends out a concert schedule every month, listing upcoming events on one side and an ad on the other. Although Tom doesn't make a great deal of money from the concerts directly, this one-of-a-kind promotion has earned the store a huge following and won him tremendous visibility in his community.

If you're clever enough to think up a great promotional sale idea, you can probably pull it off effectively. After all, the event is your personal promotion – it's your baby. Unlike the superstores, there's no chain of command for your idea to filter through and get lost like the message in a kid's game of "telephone." In addition to the kinds of community-specific events like the hootenanny at The Fret House, two kinds of promotions I've seen work well over the years are "the invitational" and "the truck-load sale."

■ **The Invitational:** Let's identify one of the most valuable assets you have in advertising: the names and addresses of your customers. Who would be more interested in what you do for a living than the people who have already done business with you? So, let them know first what's going on in your store. Postcards are cheap. Every month you should send something out to these folks to let them know what's going on. That's why they call it "direct mail." It goes directly to your customer. Advertise a special price on a single item that's been having babies in your stock room. Or talk about new arrivals: seasonal fashions, a new line of camera bags, office furniture, the latest computer technology. Promote upcoming in-store events: author readings at a bookstore, woodworking classes at a hardware store.

Offer these folks the opportunity to get in before the rest of the public on the day of the special promotional event. Address them as the "insiders," your special customers. Send them a special invitation to every special event. Don't forget to mention that they need to show the invitation in order to get in on the happenings – it implies they're special, that the event is not just for anybody. It also implies that all the goods won't be sold by the time they arrive. Plus, they'll get to rub elbows with the rest of your elite clientele.

Add a little drama by holding sales at special times. Midnight Madness sales are always fun. Close the store at six, reopen at eight, and run the sale until midnight. If you usually close at eight, begin the sale at nine. As long as you make your special event *look* special, it will be. Someone once asked me if I would let a customer in who didn't have an invitation. How absurd! I keep a pocket full of extra invitations at all times.

■ **The Truckload Sale:** "Man, we've got a truckload of this stuff. We have to get rid of it today!" Urgency always works. The trouble is, you can't take the risk of being stuck with a truckload of merchandise if your sale doesn't go over. The good news is, you don't have to afford a truckload of merchandise to hold a truckload sale. You only need to afford the truck.

> As long as you make your special event *look* special, it will be.

Call a local trucking company. Ask if they'd park one of their 30-foot trailers in front of your store for the weekend. They will charge you somewhere between free merchandise and nothing at all. Print up a 10-foot banner that shouts "TRUCKLOAD SALE" and hang it on the side of this semi-trailer. You're creating the picture of a store with so much merchandise the owners must sell it at cost.

Put tables of merchandise outside the store. This is a great opportunity to get rid of that dead stock. Tie helium balloons all over the truck and tables. Offer donuts and hot dogs. Logistics are always the hard part. Make sure everyone knows their jobs so when the crowd hits the fan, you're ready. Make sure there's plenty of parking, and music. People love music, and it makes for a more festive atmosphere.

There's got to be action at your store for an event like this to work. When people drive by, will they be able to see something is happening at your place? Even if they don't stop, they'll always remember where and who you are.

Growing up in a large family, I found it tough to be heard above the crowd. Each of us had our own loud and obnoxious way of being noticed by my own Mom and Pop. You, my friends, are members of a family of retailers – each one screaming "Me, me, me! Somebody please notice me!"

When it comes to promotions, over the top is just right. I once tried to rent an Army tank to park in front of our store. "We Blow Away the Competition!" was the promo I had in mind. Can you imagine the attention a tank would have brought to our location?! Unfortunately, the daily rate on liability insurance killed the idea. And the insurance company actually wanted security guards there to keep people off the thing. Apparently they envisioned kids climbing all over this metallic monster, breaking arms and legs and heads. It was still a great idea....

If you come up with something outrageous and people tell you you're crazy, you're probably on to something. Go for it!

Specialist Spotlight on... Clues Unlimited

For more than three decades, Patricia Davis and Christine Acevedo have lived in Tucson, Arizona – sharing a deep friendship, a passion for mystery novels... and a pot-bellied pig named Sophie. Although they would describe themselves as "born book people," neither woman ever dreamed she would one day buy a bookstore – much less a small shop specializing in a single literary category: mysteries.

Pat had been teaching English at a local community college for more than 30 years. With an MBA in finance, Chris had a successful career as a stockbroker. For both women, it was time for a change. Then, one day in 1996, an independent bookstore came on the seller's block – and the two friends plunged right in.

They changed the store's name from Footprints of a Gigantic Hound to Clues Unlimited but kept the mystery-novel theme and focus on animals. The previous owner had allowed his dogs to inhabit the store. Pat and Chris brought in Sophie as the replacement. The friendly porker has graced the shop's corner pen ever since. "You can't overestimate the effect of having animals," says Chris.

Sophie is already quite a celebrity around Tucson. Not only have numerous newspaper articles featured her, but she'll actually be starring in forthcoming mysteries by Sinclair Browning and David Cole.

People love to have their curiosity piqued – that's what makes mysteries so popular. Readers can't help turning the pages to see what happens. Curious readers come from near and far to see the bookstore pig, then stay for the books. Sophie is especially popular with the children's reading groups that visit the small two-room shop. The porky piglet loves the attention, hamming it up for her young audience and not even minding the small fingers scratching her back and exploring her nose. Ah, it's a pig's life.

The bookshop's porcine mascot is equal parts quirky charm and clever marketing strategy. And like the enquiring minds featured in their books, Pat and Chris are constantly seeking out solutions for improving that marketing. "What made this promotion work? How can we treat customers even better?" they continually ask.

They do assure me they've never thought about murdering the competition though. They'd have hundreds of customers trying to solve the crime.

Pat and Chris understand the importance of community involvement and host a variety of events, including a monthly mystery book club, author signings, and writer workshops. They sponsor the Mysteries and History benefit dinners at the University of Arizona, help fund the perennially popular *Mystery!* series on the local PBS station, and support the local chapter of Sisters in Crime, a national association of mystery fans and writers. Battling illiteracy is a pet project. And Sophie's personal favorite comes as no surprise: a fundraiser for the local pot-bellied pig sanctuary. As local retailers, these women have incredible visibility.

Such indirect marketing is only half of their business approach. Pat and Chris aggressively promote their bookstore events for free in newspaper and radio community event calendars. And they spend a whopping $9,000 – four percent of total annual sales – on producing and mailing a 24-page bimonthly newsletter to their database of 1,200 customers. Brimming with news, extensive lists of new releases in both hardcover and paperback, event schedules, and commentary, the Clues Unlimited newsletter is by no means your ordinary piece of direct mail. Extremely labor intensive to prepare, according to Chris, the new release listings are "as objective as possible" – and quite tasty too: "Sophie ate one, and she thought it was yummy."

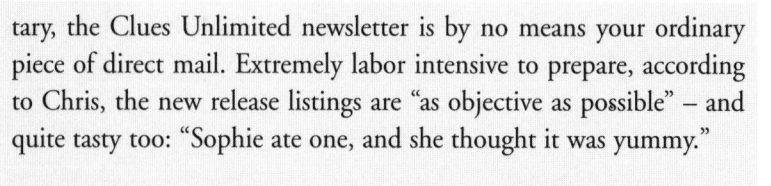

The newsletters are "worth every penny," Chris adds – driving an impressive 15 percent of their business. "Customers use them as a shopping list," explains Pat. "You'll see them with a newsletter all marked up walking about the store." It's all part of their industry's "hand selling" tradition.

In the book business, hand selling is just that. After you've interviewed your customers about their likes, you literally put the perfect book into their hands. The implication, of course, is "buy this book now!" What a great closing technique, and a great way to develop your personal trade. If you know a regular customer's tastes, you can hand her her newest purchase the moment she walks in the door. Now that's personalized service!

The ladies also print up a monthly "pick sheet," which they distribute in the shop, in mail-order fulfillment packages, and on their website. Each partner selects three or four books a month. Sophie even weighs in with her own suggestions (although there are suspicions her primary activity has to do with hiding the books on culinary arts rather than recommending them for purchase). On the rare days they have a little down time, Pat and Chris compile "genre sheets." The topics range from culinary mysteries (if you can find them) to historical who-dun-its, and everything in between.

If you've read this far in my book, you already know why these business partners are so successfully thriving in the giant's shadow. The growth of the superbookstore and online retailers did not affect their decision to buy the little book shop in the first place. So when Borders opened up two miles down the road, the question of competition never even entered their minds. Come on – the place doesn't even have a pig!

Pat and Chris did head on over to take a look, however. Not only to see what Borders was *not* doing, but to see what they're doing, and doing well. As Pat puts it, "We're not proud. We'll steal any idea – even from Borders."

She adds that their relationship with the superstores is actually quite positive. Clues Unlimited staff members routinely field questions from superstore employees and happily receive customer referrals all the time. They know that their personalized service keeps them on solid ground: "We're able to hand sell to each customer, one on one," says Chris. That's the specialist difference.

The superbookstores would love to operate the way they do at Clues Unlimited – but they can't. They'd need scores of salespeople just like Pat and Chris. Each manager would need their fiercely entrepreneurial outlook. And you're just not going to find anyone with such an outlook working for somebody else! They'd already have their own business... maybe a Wild West Clothing & Saddle Shop. With a cow roaming the aisles so customers can try out their new ropes.... Get along little doggies!

Think I'm making fun of Clues Unlimited? In a pig's eye! I'm having fun. And being successful in your own business is about as much fun as a person can have.

Chapter 11
Good News About Retailing

So, what have we learned? I hope you've come to understand that independent retailers are not simply victims of the marketplace... that you have plenty of opportunities within your reach to seek out and exploit the market niches the big-box retailers are ignoring. From Tom Seymour showing off his craftsmen in his store's front window, to Bess Steinberg offering walnut clusters to second-generation customers, to Frank Wildhaber opening up shop literally in the shadow of one of the greatest giants around, there's plenty of good news in retailing today!

I realize there are times all independent store owners feel they have no control over what they do... as if you're just standing around waiting to see what's going to happen next. It is the special person – the leader – who attempts to rise above those feelings and take the first step forward in the direction of change. Remember, the difference between fear and courage is action. Action gives you the feeling of being in control, and people in control of their lives are never victims of anything. Those people live lives filled with very little stress.

The definition of stress is "pressure without control." Now pressure *per se* is not a bad thing. We all need pressure... life itself is pressure. The knowledge that the rent must be paid creates pressure that compels us to get out of bed each morning and go to work.

If my tux is at the dry cleaners and I have an "event," I'm under pressure to get it on my way home. If I get to the cleaners and the place has closed, then I'm stressed, big time. I'll have to rent one of those tuxedos with a frilly shirt that makes me look like I belong in a polka band.

As long as you have ample time to complete a task your boss gives you, that's a "stress-free" assignment. But if the boss gives me three days' work with a one-day deadline, I'm going to be stressed. The moment circumstances hinder your completion of a project, you are no longer in control of your situation, and stress is sure to follow. A stress-free job, then, is one you're under pressure to complete, with the knowledge and confidence that you can do so.

In most cases, we can anticipate what might go wrong and head that stress off at the pass. My basic position is that Murphy was an optimist. If you special-ordered a product and promised the customer a delivery date, you'd better have a plan in place for handling the situation when the item does not show up. If you always have a "plan B," you will minimize your stress level.

Can you imagine all the people in the world who are under pressure to complete jobs they don't know how to do? We call them grumpy. They fail day after day, burn out, quit their jobs, and never have a clue what happened. Stress equals pressure without control.

Now, think of yourself trying to compete with a superstore on price and selection. It's beyond your control. You never know what their price represents because you don't buy those same items for the same amount. The stress you're putting on yourself must be enormous. You have no control over the situation!

But, if you try to compete with superstores on the things *they* cannot control, you can throw a little stress their way. It's only fair, isn't it? When the superstore thrives, so should you. If they're going to walk all those people to your store, you'd better be ready for them.

Your staff should know exactly how you want it done, why you want it done, when to do it, and how to fix it. If you teach them, make sure they know it, coach them on their performance, and write them up when they forget. You'll never worry about the superstores as competition again.

And let's never forget that the prime ingredient in any retail store should be fun. The superstore always has some kind of fun going on. If I owned a shoe store, I'd try to get me a shoe the size of a Volkswagen to put on my showroom floor. It would make people laugh. It would make them remember who I am.

If you ever have the pleasure of going to the Denver airport, look for the airplane hanging from the ceiling. A tire store near my house sports a tire two stories high. And I'm sure you've seen that L.A. donut shop that the movie industry loves to put in films: the one with the 30-foot donut outside. Silly? Sure. Fun? Absolutely. Memorable? You bet!

What can *you* do to make shopping at *your* store a memorable experience? It begins with an uninhibited love for mankind. You have to love people to be a successful retailer. After all, you're going to meet them one at a time. Yet the trend seems to be in the other direction. Shopping is becoming more impersonal. Although the Internet has been slow to turn a profit for any e-tailer, people continue to look in that direction for salvation. Like the stock market, though, these things too will become overvalued. I believe there will be an enormous backlash as to what buyers will put up with. People will simply tire of compromise.

I went recently with a friend to buy a DVD player. The salesperson told us the one he recommended had a fiber-optic output for the best sound. "I own this one myself," he said. We got home to find it had no fiber-optic output at all. When will it end? I've been working on this book for half a year and the preceding example happened the night before the manuscript was due on my editor's desk. If I were a real shopper, I could write a new chapter everyday.

I'm not angry. I'm just frustrated. I want the same thing every consumer wants: To fill my hopes, dreams, and desires. I want to go to the store, once, buy the exact right item, go home, and enjoy it. I don't want to make a dozen trips around town, wind up with a compromise, and have to console myself by saying, "At least I got a good deal!"

I did not write this book to indict the superstores of America. Having been a professional retailer myself, I stand in awe of their tremendous success. They have created a new and viable way of retailing. I wrote this book to show independent retailers the fantastic opportunity they have today. An opportunity that only exists *because* Goliath is here.

The superstores' advertising dollars bring hundreds of thousands of people into the marketplace every day. In Litchfield, Illinois, alone, the local giant gets almost 20,000 people to drive by Frank's modest appliance store every day. While those folks wander around with money in their pockets, it's more than possible they will wander into your store. Are you ready for them? Is your store cleaned? Merchandised? Are your employees ready to rock? These are questions you should ask yourself every time you put that key in the door to open up shop.

If you do everything we've talked about here, you're going to be working hard. Retail is hard. But you know something? The harder you work, the more money you make. It's always been like that, and it always will be.

Index

Acevedo, Christine 120-123
added value 31
add-on (to sales) 65-66, 77, 98
advertising
   cable 114
   and customer newsletters 121-122
   discount prices in 47
   newspaper 112, 113, 121
   radio 114-115, 121
   researching the competitions' 81
   special promotions 115-119
   strategies for specialists 56
   by superstores 111, 126
   television 114
   word-of-mouth 71, 99, 111
   Yellow Pages 112
Allied Model Trains 96-100
Amazon.com *xi*, 51
appliance store 17, 22, 68-70, 111
Arnold, Benedict 67
attitudes
   about change 23, 25, 125
   about commission 83-84
   about customer service 17-18
   and employee production 93
   about personal appearance 103-104, 106
   about price 47
   about retail 15-16
automobiles 22
banners, storefront 112

bargains, vs. versus inexpensive products 81
barter 19, 118
Best Brands Plus 69, 70
Best Buy 17
bike store 54-58, 82
BLOCKBUSTER 84
bookstore *xi*, 50-52, 111, 117, 120-123
Borders 111, 123
Boys All-Steel Velocipede 21
boxing gloves 21
Builder's Emporium 87
Bust Enlargement Cream 20
butcher 20, 29
buying group 69, 70
car stereo store 47, 106-109, *see also* hi-fi store
catalogs 21
change 25-27, 125
Circuit City 17, 22, 70
cleanliness 93-94, 99, 101-102
clothing store 29, 42
Clues Unlimited 120-123
commission 37, 83-84, 85
commitment 68
community 33, 74-75, 116
   involvement in 121
competing on price 30, 52-53, 126
complacency *xii*, 19
computer store 34-38
consumer choice *xii*, 60

convenience 33
Cordaro, Sal 34-38
cotton gin 20
Covina Valley Schwinn 54-58
Cowan, Joshua Lionel 96
credit/debit cards 29, 31, 61
cross-shopping 55, 81, 82
customer care 59-63
customer service, *see* personal trade, personalized service, self-service
   and expense 41-48
   and ignorance 48-53
customers
   commissioned sales to 84
   compromise by 127-128
   effect of staff appearance on 104
   home cooking for 77, 78
   loyalty of 33, 52, 87
   names of 29, 31, 59, 60, 62
   shopping on price 47
   and special promotions 116-117
   spillover from superstores 69-70
   surveying of 111-112
   taken for granted 63, 68, 72
   teaching of 34
   treated with politeness 60-61
   trust of *xi*, *xii*
   understanding the psyche of 26
Davis, Patricia 120-123
decor 61-62, 98-99, 101, 106-109
   and in-store signs 43

and store atmosphere 61-62, 127
department store *xi*, 17, 20, 21, 42
Di-No Computers 34-38
Disney Store, The 101
Disneyland 47, 75
dress codes 103-104
Drucker, Allen 96-100
employee *see* management, salespeople, turnover
evolution
   of a business strategy 25-27, 35
   of the marketplace 25, 29
   of retail *xi*, 17, 19-23
   of technology 34
Federated *xi*
flea markets 19, 48, 56
Fret House, The 24-27, 29, 115-116
friendship 75
fun 24, 61-62, 101, 127
furniture store 22, 72-74
gas stations 45, 46
Gillis, Dobie 31, 34
Goliath 22, 100, 128
good news 19, 47, 75, 125-128
groceries 22, 59-62
grocery store 31-33, 34, 59-62
Guitar Center 25, 111
guitars 24-27
hand selling 122
hardware store 86-88, 117 *see also* home improvement store

hay tedder 21
hi-fi store 65-66, 103
history of retailing *xi*, 19-23
hobby shop 63, 74
Home Base 87
Home Depot, The 17, 87, 111
home improvement store 17, 87, 111
IKEA 22
Industrial Revolution 20
Internet sales *xi*, 51, 63, 86, 127
inventions 20, 21, 96
inventory 22-23, 37, 88
   turns 27
jewelry store 76-78, 82-83, 96
Jones, Casey 97
Kmart *xi*, 44
L&W Appliance 68-70, 111
leaders 85, 125
leadership 67, 89-94
learning 15
   how to lead 91
   information 70
   lifelong pursuit of 66
Lionel Train company 96
liquor store 62
"Little Rascal thinking" 30
location 75, 111
   changing 27, 70, 97
Logan's Hardware 86-88
Lowe's 87
mail order 21

malls 39, 48
management
   and customer interaction 89
   and executive decisions 71
   and leadership 67, 89-94
   and paperwork 71
marketing opportunities 112-119
marketing strategies 88, 120-122, *see also* promotions
Mars Music 25
Matheson, Don 86-88
McDonald's 44-45
membership stores 46, 52, 59
Men's Wearhouse 29
merchandising 22
model ships 63
model train store 96-100
Mom and Pop 22, 29-33, 34, 38, 40, 51, 72, 87, 114
Montgomery Ward *xi*
motivating your staff 92-94
music 62, 116, 118
music store 24-27, 29, 39, 111, 115-116
Nordstrom 42
Office Depot 22
opportunity 23, 62, 67, 72, 125, 126, *see also* marketing opportunities
personal relationships
   with customers *xi*, 31, 36
   with employees 89

Index

personal trade 71-78, 122
    and how *not* to get personal with customers 72-74
    and superstore "greeters" 71
personalized service 18, 26, 29, 31-33, 36, 42-53, 56-57, 83, 98
    and commission 83-85
PetSmart 22
price(s) 15
    competing on 17, 30-31, 126
    discount 22, 41-42, 43, 46, 48, 49, 115
    researching the competitions' 81
    vs. value 79-80
price tags 80-83
product knowledge 24-25, 57, 88
product returns 21, 40, 43
product selection 22, 79, 97-99
    superstore versus specialist 88, 100
production and demand 20
products
    defining the value of 79-82
    new to market *xi*
profit center 26, 37, 98
promotions 115-119
    holiday sales 115
    hootenanny 115-116
    the invitational 116-117
    Midnight Madness sale 117
    superstore vs. specialist 116
    the "truckload" sale 117-118
qualifying the customer 77, 84-85

repair service, personalized 26, 36, 57
retail experience 30
Ritz-Carlton Hotels, The 17-18
Roth, Wes and Richard 54-58
sales slump 69, 70, 87
salespeople 19-20, 64-67
    manners of 61
    pushy vs. assertive 84-85
    and specialist knowledge 79-80, 82, 83
    using the "up system" 73
    writing notes to customers 78
Sam Ash 25
Sam's Club 52
Sears Roebuck & Co. *xi*, 17, 20, 21
self-service 44-45, 46
Seymour, Tom 24-27, 115-116, 125
sewing machines 20
Shapiro, Gary *xiii*
shoemaker 20
shopping habits
    buying on price 47, 53
    male vs. female 81
signs, *see also* banners
    in-store 43
    storefront 111, 112
specialist *xii*, 16, 19, 23, 29, 53, 67, 70, 80, 92, 100, 111, 115, *see also* personal trade, personalized service
sporting goods store 30, 56, 74 *see also* bike store

store blindness 101-102
store design 98, *see also* decor
stress 125-126
success
   and new businesses 72
   and fun 24
supermarket 29, 59-60
superstore(s) 16-17, 30, 36, 37
   characteristics of 22, 40-41
   community events at 74-75
   effect on local markets 25, 87
   forced out of market by specialists 99-100
   high-end products at 79, 82
   historically first 21-22
   increasing specialists' business 26, 57, 69-70, 88, 123
   management of 39-40
   market share of 22
   merchandising strategies of 25, 40-41
   pricing strategies of 87-88
   referrals to specialists by 88, 123
   slowness to adapt 29
   success of 17, 126, 128
   vs. big-box retailers 22
televisions 29
tire store 52-53, 67, 127
toy store 56, 63, 101
Toys "R" Us 56, 63
training *xi*, 24, 90
   in customer care 50-52, 59-63
   by manufacturers 69
   materials 66-67
   in sales 64-67
   at superstores 48, 61
traveling salesmen 21
turnover 16, 24, 35, 39
   and personal trade 71
unequal, vs. the superstores 67, 70, 72, 101-104
value 47
video store 63, 84
volume 80
Wal-Mart *xi*, 17, 29, 44, 56, 69, 70
Ward, Aaron Montgomery 21
washboards 86, 113
washing machines 29
wholesale 20
Wildhaber, Frank 68-70, 111, 125
Wylie, Steve 36

The Armarium Press.

Scribes and scholars of the ancient world would store a valuable scroll or codex in an *armarium,* the precursor to the modern bookcase. Just as the *armaria* protected those early works of learning, we at The Armarium Press aim to preserve some of the oldest traditions of book publishing.

The small creatures from the woodcut seen on our endpapers stand for speed (the butterfly) and steadfastness (the crab). During the Renaissance, the earliest commercial printers used these and similar symbols to represent the Latin phrase *festina lente,* which we have taken for our motto. Translated as "make haste slowly," these words embody the spirit with which we publish our books.